W9-AOJ-196

Carlo Goldoni's

Villeggiatura
Trilogy

Carlo Goldoni's
Villeggiatura Trilogy

translated by Robert Cornthwaite

Great Translations for Actors Series

SK
A Smith and Kraus Book

A Smith and Kraus Book
Published by Smith and Kraus, Inc.
One Main Street, PO Box 127, Lyme, NH 03768

Copyright © 1994 by Robert Cornthwaite
All rights reserved

Cover and Text Design By Julia Hill
Manufactured in the United States of America

CAUTION: Professionals and amateurs are hereby warned that CARLO GOLDONI'S VILLEGGIATURA TRILOGY is subject to a royalty. It is fully protected under the copyright laws of the United States of America, and of all countries covered by the International Copyright Union (including the Dominion of Canada and the rest of the British Commonwealth), and of all countries covered by the Pan-American Copyright Convention and the Universal Copyright Convention and of all countries with which the United States has reciprocal copyright relations. All rights, including professional, amateur, motion picture, recitation, lecturing, public reading, radio broadcasting, television, video or sound taping, all other forms of mechanical or electronic reproductions such as information storage and retrieval systems and photocopying, and the rights of translation into foreign languages, are strictly reserved. All inquiries should be addressed to Smith and Kraus, Inc.

Cover illustration: *Love Letters*, by Fragonard. © The Frick Collection. Reprinted by permission of The Frick Collection, New York, NY.

First Edition: November 1994
10 9 8 7 6 5 4 3 2 1

Library of Congress Cataloging-in-Publication Data

Cornthwaite, Robert, 1917—
    Carlo Goldoni's Villeggiatura : a trilogy / condensed, translated by Robert Cornthwaite.
    --1st ed.
    p. cm. -- (Young actors series, Great translations for actors.)
    ISBN 1-880399-72-5 : $19.95
    1. City and town life--Italy--Drama. 2. Country life--Italy--Drama. 3. Marriage proposals--
Drama. 4. Goldoni, Carlo, 1707-1793. Smanie per la villeggiatura. II. Goldoni, Carlo, 1707-
1793. Avventure dalla villeggiatura. III. Goldoni, Carlo, 1707-1793. Ritorno dalla
villeggiatura. IV. Title. V. Title: Villeggiatura. VI. Series: Great translations for actors.

PS3553.0685C37   1994
852'.6--dc20   94-38078
                                                CIP

Contents

Foreword

That combination of ambition, ignorance, and bad judgment which the 1980s called yuppie seems to have existed since the beginning of civilization. Certainly Aristophanes was taking satirical swipes at the breed in his comedies of the fifth century BC, and in the first century AD Petronius Arbiter gave us in his *Satyricon* a grand display of overweening bad taste and conspicuous consumption in the set piece called Trimalchio's Feast. In 1670 Molière trotted out *Le Bourgeois Gentilhomme* to howls of recognition. So yuppiedom as the object of satire was well established in theatrical tradition before Goldoni wrote the *Villeggiatura* trilogy in 1761.

What is new about Goldoni's satire is its sweetness. The trilogy is a long play about love, lost love, love gone astray. As Giorgio Strehler points out in *Per un teatro humano* (Feltrinelli, pages 236-239), the drama here is love seen in all its aspects, in full, with nothing held back. There is emotional abandon; there are heated encounters; and the fact that everything is tempered by Goldoni's goodness and measured wisdom adds to its spell. The wisdom and goodness, in suprisingly modern fashion, melt into a profound melancholy, of something dying in silence, of quiet resignation, accepting the evil in things and in life, feeling sympathy for others, feeling the pain of wronging those who don't deserve it, the inability to communicate, to talk, and to stop talking. We are entering the world of Chekhov, in fact, a hundred years and more before the Russian laid out the boundaries of his countryside in *The Wood Demon, The Sea Gull, Uncle Vanya, The Three Sisters,* and *The Cherry Orchard.*

One of the factors in producing a play from another time—say, the eighteenth century—is the conformation of the theater itself in that earlier day. By the time of Carlo Goldoni (1707-1793) the "wooden O" of Shakespeare had given way to the proscenium arch and the picture stage. That stage was often raked and equipped with slots to hold the wings on either side. These wings were open, whether the scene represented was exterior or interior. For this reason, the advent of a character in a Goldoni comedy is often remarked by someone onstage before that character actually enters. In *Crazy for the Country*, scene two, for instance:

> BRIGIDA: I think I hear somebody.
>
> GIACINTA: Go see who it is.
>
> BRIGIDA: Oh! It's Signor Leonardo.

Note that Brigida does not leave the stage to ascertain this information. Giacinta continues:

> GIACINTA: Why doesn't he come on it?
>
> BRIGIDA: What if he has heard about Signor Guglielmo?
>
> GIACINTA: He has to know sooner or later.
>
> BRIGIDA: He's not coming in. Something's wrong. Shall I go see?
>
> GIACINTA: Yes, see what it is and send him in.
>
> (*Brigida goes out. After a moment Leonardo enters.*)

Goldoni has taken advantage of a convention of the eighteenth century theater to build the suspense before Leonardo's entrance. The modern director will have to find a modern path toward an equivalent. Will Brigida peek through a curtain or a keyhole? The audience of 1761 accepted without question a room equipped not with solid walls but with wings like huge vertical louvers between which a character onstage could see quite clearly a character offstage. Why not? The audience could discern the open spaces between the wings; why shouldn't the actors onstage see through them too?

•

A note on the format: Goldoni divided the three comedies of the trilogy into three acts each. So that a director in today's theater can set his intermission—one pause in the performance being the custom nowadays—at the most convenient spot in a version somewhat shortened, we have left each play divided into scenes numbered from one to six, in conformity with the divisions in *Carlo Goldoni's Villeggiatura Trilogy Condensed for Young Actors*, also published by Smith and Kraus, Inc.

•

Readers will notice that Paolo's name becomes Paolino in the second play. Apparently Goldoni forgot that he had begun the trilogy with the proper name and then switched to the diminutive, just as he forgot that he had given Filippo one surname in the first play and another in the third. This translation goes with the latter—at the toss of a coin!

Carlo Goldoni's
Villeggiatura
Trilogy

Characters of *Crazy for the Country*

LEONARDO
in love with Giacinta

PAOLO
steward to Leonardo

VITTORIA
sister of Leonardo

CECCO
servant to Leonardo

BERTO
another servant to Leonardo

FERDINANDO
a free-loader

FILIPPO
a citizen, old and jovial

GUGLIELMO
in love with Giacinta

GIACINTA
daughter of Filippo

BRIGIDA
maid to Giacinta

FULGENZIO
an old friend of Filippo

TIME: *Late summer 1761.*

PLACE: *Livorno, partly in Leonardo's house and partly in Filippo's.*

Villeggiatura

Part One: Crazy for the Country

Scene 1

A room in Leonardo's house.
Paolo is packing a trunk with clothes and linens.

Leonardo enters hurriedly.

LEONARDO: What are you doing? There are a hundred things to get ready while you're wasting time in here and nothing gets done!

PAOLO: Pardon. I thought packing the trunk was necessary for your trip.

LEONARDO: I need you for something more important. Leave the packing to the women.

PAOLO: They're all busy helping the mistress and can't be bothered.

LEONARDO: That sister of mine is never happy until she has all the servants waiting on her. Two maids working for a month to get her ready for a few weeks in the country! It's insufferable!

PAOLO: She says two maids were not enough. She called in two more women to help out.

LEONARDO: What does she do with so many? Are they making her another dress?

PAOLO: No, the tailor is doing that. The women are refurbishing last year's clothes and making capes and mantles. Nowadays people dress up more in the country than they do in town.

LEONARDO: Well, we have to keep up with the crowd. Everyone goes to the country for the fall; I'm going myself. You'll have to help if we're to leave on time.

PAOLO: What can I do?

LEONARDO: First let's go over the list again. I'm afraid we're short of silverware.

PAOLO: Two dozen settings ought to be enough.

LEONARDO: For everyday use, yes, just for us. But how about guests who drop in unexpectedly? In the country we keep open house. It's best to be prepared.

PAOLO: Forgive me if I speak too freely, but there's no need to live like a lord.

LEONARDO: And there's no need for lectures!

PAOLO: Pardon. I'll say no more.

LEONARDO: My country place is next to Signor Filippo's, and he entertains on a grand scale. I refuse to look cheap in comparison. Go to Monsieur Gurland's and rent me some silverware, some cups and saucers, and six candlesticks.

PAOLO: Very well.

LEONARDO: And order ten pounds of coffee, fifty pounds of chocolate, twenty pounds of sugar, and an assortment of spices for the kitchen.

PAOLO: Do I pay cash for all this?

LEONARDO: Tell him I'll pay when I return from Montenero.

PAOLO: Excuse me, but you said the other day you expected to clear up the old bills before you left.

LEONARDO: Not now! Tell him I said later!

PAOLO: Very well.

LEONARDO: Get six or seven extra decks of cards. And don't forget candles, whatever you do.

PAOLO: The Pisa candlemaker wants the old account paid in full before he'll open a new one.

LEONARDO: Then buy Venetian candles. They cost more but they last longer.

PAOLO: For cash?

LEONARDO: Get the candles! I'll pay when I return.

PAOLO: The creditors will be yelping at your door.

LEONARDO: Paolino, you've been with me for ten years, and every year you grow more impertinent. I'm losing patience.

PAOLO: You can discharge me any time.

LEONARDO: Do what I tell you! And send Cecco here.

PAOLO: Very well.

(He leaves, standing aside for Vittoria as she enters.)

LEONARDO: Our miserly uncle could help but he won't. Well, he's bound to croak before I do, and I'm his only heir.

(Vittoria is going through the linens piled by the trunk. She finds what she wants and goes to the door but stops and lingers in the doorway when she hears Leonardo mention Guglielmo.)

(Cecco enters.)

CECCO: You wanted me?

LEONARDO: Go to Signor Filippo's and tell him with my compliments that I have ordered the horses and we'll leave together at three o'clock. Say I send my respects to his daughter Giacinta and hope she slept well last night, and I'll call on her within the hour. See if Signor Guglielmo is there by any chance. And ask the servants if he's been hanging around. Hurry back and tell me what they say.

CECCO: Very well. *(He leaves.)*

LEONARDO: I won't have Giacinta seeing Guglielmo.

VITTORIA: She says she only tolerates him to please her father. She says he's a friend of the family. She says he means nothing to her.

LEONARDO: I don't believe everything I hear. Anyhow, he rubs me the wrong way—I'd better finish packing this trunk myself.

VITTORIA: Is it true you ordered the horses for this afternoon?

LEONARDO: Yes, of course. Isn't that what we decided yesterday?

VITTORIA: Yesterday I said I *hoped* to be ready, but today I'm telling you I'm not. So cancel the horses. We absolutely cannot leave.

LEONARDO: Why not?

VITTORIA: Because my *mariage* isn't finished.

LEONARDO: What the devil is a *mariage?*

VITTORIA: My dress. It's the latest fashion.

LEONARDO: They can send it to you when it's done.

VITTORIA: No, I must try it on to make sure it fits perfectly.

LEONARDO: We can't delay. We told Signor Filippo and Giacinta we would leave with them this afternoon.

VITTORIA: I don't care. Giacinta always wears the latest fashion and I refuse to look dowdy next to her.

LEONARDO: You have lots of other dresses.

VITTORIA: Old rags!

LEONARDO: Didn't you have a new one made just last year?

VITTORIA: Clothes go out of style! I've had them done over till they're ready to fall apart. I've got to have a new dress. I've simply got to.

LEONARDO: And this year *mariage* is the style?

VITTORIA: Of course! Madame Granon was wearing one in Torino. Nobody in Livorno has even seen a *mariage* and I'll be the first.

LEONARDO: What kind of thing is it? Hard to make, I suppose.

VITTORIA: It's very simple!—silk of one color overlaid with two other colors intertwined. The trick is to choose the right colors. They must contrast but not clash. It's stunning.

LEONARDO: What can I say? I'm sorry to disappoint you, but we have to leave today.

VITTORIA: I won't go.

LEONARDO: We'll go without you.

VITTORIA: You'd have the heart to leave me behind?

LEONARDO: I'll come back for you.

VITTORIA: How can I depend on that? Heaven knows when you'll come, and if I'm left here alone I'm afraid that wheezing old uncle of ours will make me stay with him; and if I have to stay behind while everybody is away in the country, I'll die.

LEONARDO: Then make up your mind. We leave at three.

VITTORIA: No. You go to the tailor and make him drop everything and finish my *mariage*.

LEONARDO: I haven't time. I have a hundred things to do.

VITTORIA: I'll die! I warn you—I'll die!

LEONARDO: Die? For one little dress?

VITTORIA: Yes! A girl would rather die than not be in style!

LEONARDO: A girl is right! Wait till you're married.

VITTORIA: Giacinta is a girl and she's in style. She dresses just like a married woman. Nowadays nobody can tell the difference, and a girl who doesn't dress like all the others is a freak. You want people to make fun of me?

LEONARDO: All this fuss for a dress!

VITTORIA: I'd rather catch some horrible disease.

LEONARDO: I wish you luck.

VITTORIA: (*Resentfully.*) Catching a disease?

LEONARDO: No. Getting your dress and getting your way—as usual.

(Enter Berto.)

BERTO: Signor Ferdinando is calling to pay his respects.

LEONARDO: Ask him to come in.

VITTORIA: (*To Berto.*) Listen. Run to the French tailor and tell him to finish my dress right away. I want it ready before I leave for the country or else he'll have me to contend with and he'll be out in Livorno.

BERTO: Very well. (*He leaves.*)

LEONARDO: Now keep quiet about clothes and don't give yourself away in front of Ferdinando.

VITTORIA: What do I care about Ferdinando? I'm not afraid of him. He's probably come to sponge off us down in the country again this year.

LEONARDO: Of course he has. He acts as if he were doing us a favor. But since he goes everywhere and gossips about everybody you'd better watch what you say. If he knows how frantic you are about that dress, he'll ridicule you in every house he visits.

VITTORIA: The toad! Why take him with us?

LEONARDO: Look, in the country one must have company. People invite as many guests as possible. They talk about it: So-and-so has ten people, and so-and-so has only six. Whoever has the most guests is top dog. Besides, Ferdinando is useful. He's good at cards, he's cheerful and funny, he eats like a horse and makes the hostess happy, and he puts up with everything without complaint.

VITTORIA: That's true. In the country his kind are essential. What's happened to him? Why doesn't he come on in?

LEONARDO: He's probably in the kitchen.

VITTORIA: Why the kitchen?

LEONARDO: Curiosity. He likes to know what's for dinner—and then he spreads the news everywhere.

VITTORIA: Lucky for us he won't be able to tell any tales of starvation here.

(Enter Ferdinando.)

FERDINANDO: My respects to you both.

VITTORIA: Your servant.

LEONARDO: Well, friend, are you coming with us?

FERDINANDO: Yes, I'll come along. I managed to get away from that dreary Count Anselmo, who was insisting I go with his crowd.

VITTORIA: Count Anselmo! Isn't he a good host in the country?

FERDINANDO: Oh, he sets a fine table, but life in his villa is so dull. Supper at nine o'clock and to bed by ten.

VITTORIA: I wouldn't live like that for all the money in the world. If I go to bed before dawn I simply can't sleep.

LEONARDO: You know how it is with us—cards and dancing till supper at midnight—at the earliest—and then some serious gambling till the sun is up.

VITTORIA: That's the life.

FERDINANDO: You see why I prefer your company to Count Anselmo's. Besides, that ancient wife of his is insufferable.

VITTORIA: Is she still trying to play the young flirt?

FERDINANDO: Take my word! I was her beau for a few days last year— until a pretty boy of twenty-two came along and she gobbled him up.

VITTORIA: Really? Only twenty-two?

FERDINANDO: Not a day over. A curly-haired blond young thing, all pink and white as a rose.

LEONARDO: How could he stand her?

FERDINANDO: Oh, you know—one of those fellows that hang around old ladies who buy them drinks and pay their gambling debts.

VITTORIA: You have a good word for everybody.

FERDINANDO: Only for those who deserve it. Well, when do we leave?

VITTORIA: We don't know yet.

FERDINANDO: I suppose it will be a carriage for four.

LEONARDO: No, I've ordered a two-seater for my sister and me, and a saddle horse for my man.

FERDINANDO: Then how do I go?

LEONARDO: However you like.

VITTORIA: (*To Leonardo.*) Now, now, Ferdinando will come with me and you go with Signor Filippo and Giacinta. I'll not be seen traveling with my brother, for heaven's sake.

LEONARDO: (*To Vittoria.*) You have decided to go then?

FERDINANDO: Is there some doubt about it?

VITTORIA: There might be.

FERDINANDO: If you're not sure, tell me frankly. I can go with someone else. Everybody is heading for the country, and I don't want them saying I'm left to hold the fort in Livorno.

VITTORIA: That's how I feel.

(Cecco enters.)

CECCO: (*To Leonardo.*) Here I am.

LEONARDO: (*Taking Cecco aside.*) Come here. (*To Ferdinando.*) With your permission.

CECCO: (*Low.*) Signor Filippo sends his regards and says he leaves the horses to you. His daughter Giacinta is anxious to start because she doesn't like traveling after dark.

LEONARDO: (*Low.*) No word about Signor Guglielmo?

CECCO: (*Low.*) They haven't seen him this morning.

LEONARDO: (*Low.*) Good. (*To the others.*) I'm going to order the horses for two-thirty.

VITTORIA: But if that thing isn't done in time...!

LEONARDO: Either it will be or it won't, and whether you come or not, I'm leaving at two-thirty.

FERDINANDO: I'll be here, packed and ready to go.

VITTORIA: I can't go till I see you know what!

LEONARDO: I've given my word. If there were some good reason, all right; but I'm not waiting around for some rags to be delivered! (*Leonardo leaves.*)

FERDINANDO: Tell me confidentially: what's keeping you from leaving?

(Vittoria ignores the question and turns to Cecco.)

VITTORIA: Cecco.

CECCO: Yes?

VITTORIA: When you were at Signor Filippo's...

CECCO: Yes?

VITTORIA: ...did you see his daughter Giacinta?

CECCO: I saw her, yes.

VITTORIA: What was she doing?

CECCO: Trying on a dress.

VITTORIA: A new dress?

CECCO: Brand new.

VITTORIA: What was it like, this dress of Giacinta's?

CECCO: I think it was a wedding dress.

VITTORIA: A wedding dress? Was anything said about her getting married?

CECCO: Well . . . the tailor said something like that—in French.

VITTORIA: I understand French. What did he say?

CECCO: He was going on about a . . . *mariage.*

VITTORIA: He's making her a *mariage?* He's not! Where is Berto? Find Berto for me. If he's not here, you run to my tailor and tell him he has exactly three hours to deliver my *mariage.*

CECCO: Doesn't *mariage* mean . . . matrimony?

VITTORIA: Run, I said! Do what I tell you and no back talk!

CECCO: Yes. I'll run all the way. *(He leaves.)*

FERDINANDO: Tell me the truth—would you be hesitating about leaving because of a dress, by any chance?

VITTORIA: What if I were?

FERDINANDO: Oh, you have every reason in the world! A woman has to have a dress. They all do—even women you wouldn't think would care. You know Signora Costanza?

VITTORIA: Yes, of course, I know her.

FERDINANDO: She had a dress made and she's paying one crown a month on it. She sold her last two pairs of sheets and a bath towel and two dozen napkins to buy the material.

VITTORIA: What for?

FERDINANDO: For her trip to the country.

VITTORIA: I can understand that perfectly. I would do the same thing. Ferdinando, do me a favor. Come with me to my tailor and help me scream at him to hurry up.

FERDINANDO: I'll tell you how to handle him. Are you paying him today?

VITTORIA: I'll pay him when I return.

FERDINANDO: Pay him on delivery and you'll get prompt service.

VITTORIA: (*Tossing her head.*) I'll pay when I choose, and I want service when I like. (*She leaves.*)

FERDINANDO: Well, hoity-toity!

Scene 2

A room in Filippo's house.
Filippo is greeting Guglielmo as he enters.

FILIPPO: Oh, Guglielmo! How good of you to come see us off!

GUGLIELMO: Simply my duty, Signor Filippo, nothing more. I heard you were leaving for the country today, and I came to wish you a good trip and a happy vacation.

FILIPPO: Dear friend, I am much obliged. Yes, we are finally getting away. I wanted to leave a month ago. When I was a boy we went to the country just to put up the wine and then came home. Now we go for pleasure and stay on till it frosts and there's not a leaf left on the trees.

GUGLIELMO: You're the master—why not come and go as you please?

FILIPPO: I could do that. But I like company. I hate to be alone, and if I went earlier, not a dog would follow me out of town. Nobody wants to be in the country by himself; it's a bore. Even my daughter makes a sour face when we're left alone together—and my Giacinta is all I have. To please her we go when the others go. I let them decide.

GUGLIELMO: Yes, the majority rules. We really must concede they know best.

FILIPPO: Not always, not always. A lot could be said on both sides. Where are you spending your vacation?

GUGLIELMO: I don't know yet.

FILIPPO: Your father used to go to the hills above Pisa.

GUGLIELMO: Yes, we have land there and a passable house. But I am single and, as you say, being alone in the country means a slow death from boredom.

FILIPPO: Want to come with us?

GUGLIELMO: Oh, Signor Filippo! I wouldn't impose!

FILIPPO: Don't stand on ceremony. I can accept the modern style in everything but these fussy qualms and compliments. If you'd like to come, I can offer you a good bed, food that's not too bad, and a heart always at the disposal of my friends.

GUGLIELMO: I don't know what to say. You are so obliging I cannot refuse.

FILIPPO: Done, then. Come and stay as long as you like. You can leave whenever you feel you must, but do stay as long as you're having a good time.

GUGLIELMO: When are you leaving?

FILIPPO: I don't know. Take that up with Leonardo.

GUGLIELMO: Leonardo is coming with you?

FILIPPO: Yes, we've arranged to travel with him and his sister. Their villa in Montenero is near ours so we're all going together.

GUGLIELMO: I see.

FILIPPO: Something wrong?

GUGLIELMO: Oh no. Since I'm alone, I was wondering if I should take a carriage or hire a saddle horse.

FILIPPO: Come in our carriage. There are only three of us and there's room for four. You'll come with us.

GUGLIELMO: Who else is coming along?

FILIPPO: My widowed sister Sabina. Not that Giacinta needs a chaperone —my daughter is a level-headed girl—but since her mother's gone, for the sake of appearances there has to be an older woman around.

GUGLIELMO: I must take pains to captivate this dear old lady with my charms!

FILIPPO: So . . . you don't mind coming?

GUGLIELMO: Mind? It's the kindest invitation I could possibly receive!

FILIPPO: Then go tell Leonardo to save that seat for you.

GUGLIELMO: Perhaps you could kindly send word to him.

FILIPPO: My servants are all busy with the move. Is there a problem?

GUGLIELMO: No, I simply had a little business to attend to. Never mind, I'll go tell him. Signor Filippo, I'll see you very soon.

FILIPPO: Don't keep us waiting.

GUGLIELMO: I shall be prompt. (*Giacinta enters. Guglielmo sees her and bows. She nods in return and sweeps on by to her father as Guglielmo follows her with his eyes.*) Believe me, I have every reason to be on time.

(He bows again and leaves.)

GIACINTA: Father, I need some money.

FILIPPO: What for this time?

GIACINTA: My silk duster.

FILIPPO: My pocket is a bottomless well. But does your duster have to be silk?

(Brigida enters and goes to Giacinta with the silk duster.)

GIACINTA: Absolutely. Silk—with a hood. *(She models the duster for her father.)*

FILIPPO: What's the hood for?

GIACINTA: At night, when it's windy or wet or cold.

FILIPPO: Wear a bonnet.

GIACINTA: Oh, a bonnet!

BRIGIDA: *(Laughing.)* Ho, ho, ho! A bonnet!

GIACINTA: Can you imagine, Brigida? A bonnet?

BRIGIDA: Your father is very amusing. A bonnet!

FILIPPO: What did I say that's so funny? Don't they wear bonnets?

GIACINTA: Father, you're hopeless. Bonnets are out.

BRIGIDA: They're antique.

FILIPPO: When did they stop wearing bonnets?

GIACINTA: Oh, two years ago, at least.

FILIPPO: In two years they've become antique?

BRIGIDA: What's in one year is out the next.

GIACINTA: And men are worse than women. They wear dusters too, and brilliants on their shoe buckles, and satin breeches to travel in.

BRIGIDA: But walking sticks are out.

GIACINTA: And daggers are in.

BRIGIDA: Some men carry parasols.

GIACINTA: And they complain about us!

FILIPPO: It's beyond me. I only know the way it was fifty years ago. That's how it will always be for me.

GIACINTA: Then there's no use talking. Please let me have some money.

FILIPPO: I see spending is still in.

GIACINTA: Father, I confine myself to the barest necessities.

FILIPPO: Well, necessities or not, I want to please my dear daughter. My purse is on my dresser. Go take the money you need. But learn a little economy. It won't be easy to find a husband as soft as your father.

GIACINTA: When are we leaving?

FILIPPO: At three, I think.

GIACINTA: Oh, earlier than that surely! Who will be in the carriage with us?

FILIPPO: Your aunt and I and a friend of mine.

GIACINTA: Some old man?

FILIPPO: Would you be sorry if it were an old man?

GIACINTA: Oh, I don't care as long as he doesn't go to sleep and snore.

FILIPPO: He's a young man.

BRIGIDA: Much better. Young people are livelier and wittier. You have a good time and you don't go to sleep on the way.

GIACINTA: Who is he?

FILIPPO: Guglielmo, who just left.

GIACINTA: Oh yes. He's all right.

FILIPPO: I expect Leonardo will ride in the carriage with his sister.

GIACINTA: Probably.

BRIGIDA: And who will I go with?

FILIPPO: You'll go by boat, as usual, with my servants and Signor Leonardo's.

BRIGIDA: But I get seasick! Last year I nearly died! I don't want to go near a boat again!

FILIPPO: You expect me to hire a carriage especially for you?

BRIGIDA: Forgive me, but who is going with Signor Leonardo's man?

GIACINTA: That's right. Leonardo's manservant is traveling by land. Let poor Brigida go with him.

FILIPPO: With the manservant?

GIACINTA: Yes. What's there to fear? You know Brigida is a good girl.

BRIGIDA: I'll just climb in and go to sleep. I swear I won't even look at a soul.

GIACINTA: It's only right I should take my maid along.

BRIGIDA: All the ladies do.

GIACINTA: There are a hundred things I might need along the way.

BRIGIDA: And I'll be right there to help you.

GIACINTA: Dear father!

BRIGIDA: Dear Signor Filippo!

FILIPPO: Dear, dear, dear . . . I don't know what to say. I can't say no—I never learned how. (*He leaves.*)

GIACINTA: Happy now?

BRIGIDA: You're very good to me.

GIACINTA: I'm good at one thing: I can get my way when I want it.

BRIGIDA: But what will Signor Leonardo say?

GIACINTA: About what?

BRIGIDA: About Signor Guglielmo going along. You know how jealous he is. If he sees him in the carriage with you . . .

GIACINTA: He'll have to put up with it.

BRIGIDA: I'm afraid he'll be angry.

GIACINTA: With Guglielmo?

BRIGIDA: With you.

GIACINTA: Of course he will, but I have made him put up with worse things.

BRIGIDA: The poor man loves you so.

GIACINTA: I have nothing against him.

BRIGIDA: He wants so much for you to marry him.

GIACINTA: I might.

BRIGIDA: Then let him know somehow, poor fellow.

GIACINTA: Oh no. If he's going to be my husband, I must train him not to be jealous and demanding. Otherwise he'll encroach on my freedom. If he once begins to think he can tell me what to do, it's all over; I'll be a slave for life. Either he loves me or he doesn't. If he loves me he has to trust me. If he doesn't, let him go his own way.

BRIGIDA: But they say jealousy is a sign of love.

GIACINTA: That kind of love is not for me.

BRIGIDA: Just between the two of us, you don't love Signor Leonardo very much.

GIACINTA: I really don't know . . . I like him more than the other men here in Livorno, and I wouldn't mind marrying him—but not if I have to be tormented by jealousy.

BRIGIDA: That's not true love, I'm afraid.

GIACINTA: I can't help it. It's the best I can do.

BRIGIDA: I think I hear somebody.

GIACINTA: Go see who it is.

BRIGIDA: Oh! It's Signor Leonardo.

GIACINTA: Why doesn't he come on in?

BRIGIDA: What if he has heard about Signor Guglielmo?

GIACINTA: He has to know sooner or later.

BRIGIDA: He's not coming in. Something's wrong. Shall I go see?

GIACINTA: Yes, see what it is and send him in.

(Brigida goes out. After a moment Leonardo enters.)

LEONARDO: (*Cool and reserved.*) Your servant.

GIACINTA: (*Equally reserved.*) Your humble servant.

LEONARDO: Pardon me if I intrude.

GIACINTA: (*Ironically.*) Please! Such ceremony!

LEONARDO: I came to wish you a good journey.

GIACINTA: Where?

LEONARDO: To the country.

GIACINTA: You're not favoring us with your company?

LEONARDO: No.

GIACINTA: May I know why?

LEONARDO: You have other company. I wouldn't want to be in the way.

GIACINTA: You're never in the way. You're always welcome because you're so cheerful and so charming.

LEONARDO: I am not the one who is charming. The charming one will be with you in your carriage.

GIACINTA: I didn't make the arrangements. My father did, and he has the right to invite anyone he likes.

LEONARDO: And his daughter doesn't object. Well, I do.

GIACINTA: That's not up to you.

LEONARDO: Frankly, I don't approve of these arrangements, as you call them.

GIACINTA: Don't tell me about it.

LEONARDO: Who then?

GIACINTA: Talk to my father.

LEONARDO: I can't go whining to him about a thing like this.

GIACINTA: And I can't compel him.

LEONARDO: If my affection means anything to you, you will find a way not to upset me.

GIACINTA: How? Just tell me how.

LEONARDO: You always find pretexts when you want to.

GIACINTA: Such as?

LEONARDO: For example . . . something happens to postpone your leaving. If you have to, you could abandon the trip altogether rather than upset someone you care about.

GIACINTA: Yes, if I wanted to look like a fool, that would be the way to do it.

LEONARDO: Ah! You mean you don't care about me.

GIACINTA: I like you, I respect you, but I won't look ridiculous because of you.

LEONARDO: Would it be such a disaster, not to go to the country for once?

GIACINTA: Not go to the country! What would people say? I couldn't look my friends in the face. People would laugh at me!

LEONARDO: If that's how it is, there's nothing to be said. Go, have a marvelous time, and much good may it do you!

GIACINTA: You'll be coming too.

LEONARDO: Oh no, I won't.

GIACINTA: (*Wheedling.*) Oh yes, you will.

LEONARDO: I don't want to be anywhere near him.

GIACINTA: What has he done to you?

LEONARDO: I can't stand the sight of him.

GIACINTA: Then you must hate him more than you love me.

LEONARDO: I hate him because I love you.

GIACINTA: Why?

LEONARDO: Because . . . because . . . Don't make me say it.

GIACINTA: Because you're jealous?

LEONARDO: Yes. Because I'm jealous.

GIACINTA: There! That's what I mean! Your jealousy is an insult to me! You couldn't be jealous of him unless you think I'm flighty and a flirt. Where there is respect for a person there is no room for such thoughts. And if there is no respect there's no love. If you don't love me, then leave me alone; and if you don't know how to love, then learn. I like you and I'm faithful to you and I'm sincere and I know what's proper and I don't want jealousy and spite and I won't be ridiculed by anybody. Besides, I'm going to the country! I have to!

LEONARDO: You're not going to the country. I'll see to that.

GIACINTA: (*Overlapping.*) I must go!

LEONARDO: Damn the country! That's where all this started! That's where you met him!

GIACINTA: (*Overlapping.*) What will people say? I will go!

LEONARDO: (*Overlapping.*) I don't care what people say! I don't care what my sister says! Nobody's going to the country!

(She leaves in one direction, he in the other.)

Scene 3

The room in Leonardo's house.
Vittoria and Paolo.

VITTORIA: Stop fussing. Go away and let the women get on with their work. I'll help you finish packing my brother's trunk later.

PAOLO: With all these servants I don't see why I have to do everything.

VITTORIA: Hurry! We must be ready when Leonardo returns. By noon my new dress will be here. Oh, I'm so happy!

PAOLO: The tailor finished it?

VITTORIA: Yes, finally. But I'll never go to him again.

PAOLO: Why? Did he do a bad job?

VITTORIA: No, It's lovely. It fits perfectly. It's in wonderful taste. They'll all be looking at me. My friends will die of envy.

PAOLO: Then why are you angry with the tailor?

VITTORIA: Because. He insisted on payment before he would deliver it.

PAOLO: Forgive me, but I don't think he was unfair. He informed me several times he was already out a lot of money for materials and seamstresses for your dress.

VITTORIA: Well, he should have simply added it to the bill. Then he would have been paid for everything all at once.

PAOLO: When?

VITTORIA: After we return from the country.

PAOLO: Do you expect to return with money?

VITTORIA: I might. In the country we play cards for high stakes and I'm very lucky. I could probably pay the tailor's bill without touching the pittance my brother allows me for clothes.

PAOLO: Well, now it's paid for and you don't have to worry.

VITTORIA: But it leaves me with no money!

PAOLO: You won't need money in the country.

VITTORIA: How can I bet at cards? I'm mad about playing faro! I have to play . . . and I have to win! If I'm not in the game they'll all wonder why. Anyhow, I'm depending on you.

PAOLO: On me?

VITTORIA: Yes, of course. For an advance against my allowance.

PAOLO: I'm sorry. You have had over half of it already.

VITTORIA: What's the difference? It will be mine anyhow. I didn't think you'd make me beg for it.

PAOLO: I would gladly help you out if I had it. Your brother put me in charge of the household expenses, but you and he spend more than comes in. I haven't drawn my own wages for six months.

VITTORIA: I'll tell my brother. He'll let me have it.

PAOLO: Believe me, he hasn't got it.

VITTORIA: He will when they harvest the wheat.

PAOLO: They won't harvest enough for our bread.

VITTORIA: Well, the grapes will bring in some money.

PAOLO: Your brother has sold the grapes in advance.

VITTORIA: Sold all the grapes? But not my uncle's.

PAOLO: Oh, your uncle has plenty of everything—grain and wine . . . and money.

VITTORIA: Then can't we get a little something from him?

PAOLO: He keeps his property separate. He likes it that way. Don't hope for anything there.

VITTORIA: You mean my brother will have nothing coming in?

PAOLO: Not unless something is done.

VITTORIA: Like what?

PAOLO: Your brother must cut expenses. Change the way you live. Above all, give up these costly vacations in the country.

VITTORIA: Give up the country? You don't know what you're saying! We can cut down on expenses and entertaining in town if we have to, yes —reduce the household staff—or cut their wages. We can spend less money here in Livorno. But not in the country, no! We must keep up appearances.

PAOLO: How long can that go on?

VITTORIA: Let it last while I'm here, that's all I ask. My dowry is safe in trust, and I hope to be married before long.

PAOLO: And in the meanwhile?

VITTORIA: Meanwhile let's finish packing.

PAOLO: Here's your brother.

VITTORIA: Now don't say anything to upset him. I want him in a good mood when we leave. Let's finish packing the trunk.

(The two of them hasten to repack the trunk. Leonardo enters.)

VITTORIA: We're hard at work, brother, packing for you.

LEONARDO: There's no hurry. We're not leaving today.

VITTORIA: We have to! I'm ready; my *mariage* is finished, I'm very happy with it, and I can't wait to go.

LEONARDO: I cancelled the horses. I thought you'd be pleased.

VITTORIA: Cancel the cancellation! Let's go!

LEONARDO: Today it's impossible.

VITTORIA: All right—tomorrow early. We'll leave then. Won't we?

LEONARDO: I don't know. I'm not sure yet.

VITTORIA: You want me to do something desperate?

LEONARDO: I can't prevent you.

VITTORIA: You must have a reason!

LEONARDO: Well, it's not some new dress, I can tell you that.

VITTORIA: Is Giacinta still planning to leave this afternoon?

LEONARDO: She may not go either.

VITTORIA: Aha! There's your reason! That's it! Because Beauty isn't leaving, her beau won't go either. Well, Giacinta doesn't run my life.

We'll leave without her.

LEONARDO: We'll leave when I decide to leave.

VITTORIA: You can't do this to me! I won't stay in Livorno when everybody is going to Montenero. Giacinta will hear from me. She'll be sorry if I'm left here because of her. I'll beat my head against the wall!

LEONARDO: Be reasonable. (*To Paolo.*) What are you standing there for like a stick?

PAOLO: I'm waiting for orders. Do I pack or do I start unpacking?

VITTORIA: Go on packing.

LEONARDO: Start unpacking.

PAOLO: (*Taking out clothes.*) It's all the same to me. They're both a lot of work.

VITTORIA: I'd like to throw everything out the window!

LEONARDO: Start with your *mariage.*

VITTORIA: I will! If I don't go to the country, I'll tear it to pieces!

LEONARDO: (*To Paolo.*) What's in this chest?

PAOLO: Coffee, chocolate, sugar, candles, and spices.

LEONARDO: Are they paid for?

PAOLO: How could they be? I had to go down on my knees to get anything at all. The shopkeepers treated me like a robber.

LEONARDO: Take them back and get credit for them.

PAOLO: Very well. (*Calling.*) Hey! Anybody there to give me a hand?

(Cecco and Berto enter to carry out the chest.)

VITTORIA: Well, there goes our stay in the country.

PAOLO: Good for you, Signor Leonardo. Reduce the debts as much as possible.

LEONARDO: Don't you lecture me!

PAOLO: (*To the servants.*) Come along before he changes his mind.

(Paolo goes out with Cecco and Berto, who carry the chest.)

VITTORIA: Why are you in such a filthy mood?

LEONARDO: I don't know why myself.

VITTORIA: Have you quarreled with Giacinta?

LEONARDO: Forget Giacinta! She's no friend of ours and I order you not to go near her.

VITTORIA: I knew it! I'm never wrong. We're not going to the country because of that hussy. If she goes and I don't, everybody will laugh at me.

LEONARDO: She'll not go either. I'll see to that.

VITTORIA: Then I wouldn't mind so much. But if she does—if she's living like a duchess in Montenero and I'm stuck in town, I'll . . . I'll beat my head against the wall!

LEONARDO: She can't go. I cancelled the horses.

VITTORIA: (*Sarcastically.*) Oh, of course they could never order more!

LEONARDO: I did something else too. I told Signor Filippo that if he's wise he won't take his daughter to the country.

VITTORIA: I'm glad! She'll have to wear her grand new *mariage* in

Livorno! I'll watch her parade it around on the docks! I'll do down and laugh in her face!

LEONARDO: I don't want you talking to her.

VITTORIA: Don't worry. I can sneer without talking.

(Enter Ferdinando dressed for travel.)

FERDINANDO: Here I am, ready to go.

VITTORIA: *(Dryly.)* You're early.

LEONARDO: Dear friend, I'm terribly sorry. Because of urgent business I'm not leaving today.

FERDINANDO: Oh diamine! When are you going? Tomorrow?

LEONARDO: I'm not sure. We may have to wait a few days. It might even be that business will keep me from going to the country at all.

FERDINANDO: Oh you poor devil!

VITTORIA: I know. It puts me in a cold sweat.

LEONARDO: You could go with Count Anselmo.

FERDINANDO: Don't worry. I'll get to Montenero without Count Anselmo. I'll go with Signor Filippo and Giacinta.

VITTORIA: Giacinta may not go this year either.

FERDINANDO: Oh yes, she will. I just came from there. They're ready to leave. Horses ordered for two o'clock.

VITTORIA: You hear, Leonardo?

FERDINANDO: They don't scrimp in that house. Signor Filippo lives like a lord. Business doesn't keep him from going to the country.

VITTORIA: You hear, Leonardo?

LEONARDO: I hear, I hear! And I get your sarcasm, Ferdinando. You've been a guest in my house many, many times—here in the city and in the country as well—and you haven't starved to death so far. If I don't go to the country, it's because I have my own reasons for it and I don't have to explain them to anybody. Go any way you like and don't bother coming to me. (*He storms out.*)

FERDINANDO: Has your brother gone mad? What have I done to him?

VITTORIA: You made it sound as if we hadn't the money to go to the country.

FERDINANDO: I did? I'm amazed. You're my friends. I'd lay down my life . . . I'd defend your reputation, sword in hand. If Leonardo has business in Livorno, why should he have to go to the country? If I said Signor Filippo doesn't scrimp, I meant it's because Signor Filippo is a crazy old man who neglects his business and squanders his money; and his daughter is worse than he is. I respect Leonardo's prudence and economy, just as I respect yours. You do what you can afford to do. Let other people ruin themselves if that's what they want.

VITTORIA: But you must wonder why. You know my brother isn't staying in Livorno out of dire poverty.

FERDINANDO: No, no, no. I know that. It's simple need.

VITTORIA: Need! What do you mean?

FERDINANDO: Need to tend to business. That's all.

VITTORIA: And Giacinta—you think she's going to the country?

FERDINANDO: Oh, no doubt about it.

VITTORIA: You're sure?

FERDINANDO: Absolutely. I saw her new dress.

VITTORIA: Is it nice?

FERDINANDO: Magnificent.

VITTORIA: Better than mine?

FERDINANDO: Better than yours? Oh, I don't say that, but it's simply gorgeous. It will be the talk of the countryside. You know, it's going to be a marvelous season this year.

VITTORIA: You think so?

FERDINANDO: Everyone will be there, all the ladies in splendid dresses; and ladies attract all the young men, you know; and where there's youth everything goes swimmingly. There'll be wonderful card parties, fantastic fancy balls . . . It will be madly amusing. I can hardly wait. Well, goodbye for now.

VITTORIA: Your servant.

FERDINANDO: Can I do anything for you at Montenero?

VITTORIA: Who knows? We may meet there.

FERDINANDO: If you come, of course we will. If not, we'll drink a toast to you.

VITTORIA: Don't go to all that trouble.

FERDINANDO: Here's to fair weather! Here's to happiness! Here's to the country! Your most humble servant.

VITTORIA: My devoted respects. (*He leaves.*) Damnation!

Scene 4

The room in Filippo's house.
Filippo and Brigida.

BRIGIDA: Signor Leonardo will not leave with us this afternoon?

FILIPPO: That was the message he sent. Perhaps something came up, I don't know. What astounded me was that he cancelled the horses not only for himself but for me too, as if he was afraid I wouldn't pay for them and he would be stuck with the bill. I didn't expect that kind of rudeness from him.

BRIGIDA: Have you decided what to do?

FILIPPO: I can get horses without Leonardo. I've already ordered some for today.

BRIGIDA: How many, may I ask?

FILIPPO: The usual— four for my carriage.

BRIGIDA: How about me?

FILIPPO: You'll have to go by boat.

BRIGIDA: On the sea again? I absolutely cannot! Isn't Signor Ferdinando coming with you?

FILIPPO: Yes. He had planned to go with Signor Leonardo, but he dropped by a little while ago to say he was coming with us.

BRIGIDA: Then you'll have to pay his way, won't you?

FILIPPO: Why?

BRIGIDA: Because when you bring out architects and builders and surveyors to work for you, you pay their way, don't you? You ought to do the same for Signor Ferdinando, because he comes with you to the country for business too: he comes to eat. And if you bring him along, it would cost nothing to bring me. Since I'm not going in the carriage with Signor Leonardo's man, I can go in the carriage with Signor Free-Loader.

FILIPPO: You make a good case. All right, if I must provide a carriage for Signor Ferdinando Free-Loader, there's room for Signora Brigida Sharp-Tongue. Who's out in the hall?

BRIGIDA: I'll see. (*After looking off.*) It's Signor Fulgenzio.

FILIPPO: Looking for me?

BRIGIDA: Probably.

FILIPPO: Go see what he wants.

BRIGIDA: Who knows? He may be another guest eager to pay you his humble respects and share your table in the country.

FILIPPO: With him it would be a pleasure. I owe him a lot, and in the country I turn no one away.

BRIGIDA: Then you'll never lack company. Where there are crumbs the birds will gather, and where there is a bountiful table the free-loaders flock.

(*She leaves as Giacinta hurries in.*)

GIACINTA: He might choose a better time to call! We're leaving at two, I have to change clothes, and we haven't eaten yet.

FILIPPO: I must see what Fulgenzio wants.

GIACINTA: Send word you're busy and haven't time to talk.

FILIPPO: How can I say that? He's an old friend.

GIACINTA: Then cut it short.

FILIPPO: As short as I can.

GIACINTA: He'll talk all day.

FILIPPO: Shush! Here he is.

GIACINTA: I'm going. (*She hurries out.*)

FILIPPO: These girls!

(Fulgenzio enters.)

FULGENZIO: Good morning, Filippo.

FILIPPO: Well, my dear old Fulgenzio! What good wind brings you here?

FULGENZIO: I wanted to see you before you left for the country.

FILIPPO: Why don't you come with us?

FULGENZIO: No, old friend, thank you very much. I was in Montenero for the harvest, again for the spring planting, I was back for the haying, and I'll be there for the winemaking. But I'm used to going alone and staying just long enough to take care of business and no longer.

FILIPPO: I love the country, and I love company.

FULGENZIO: That's fine. Wonderful. Company is fine . . . as long as it's decent.

FILIPPO: Fulgenzio, you seem to have something—or someone—in mind.

FULGENZIO: You're a dear friend to me, you know. And over the years I've tried to be a friend to you.

FILIPPO: I know, and I'll always be grateful. When I've needed money, you've always helped out. And I've always paid you back, haven't I? The thousand crowns I borrowed the other day will be returned to you in three months, as we agreed.

FULGENZIO: I'm sure of that. Lending a thousand crowns is nothing. But allow me to share something. I have noticed you come to me for a loan almost every year when it's time to go to the country. That's a sign these vacations are really too much for you. It's a shame that a fine upstanding man like you should have to borrow money to throw away. Yes—throw away. Because the same people who eat at your table are the first to gossip about you, and among those you treat so generously there's one who threatens your family's name and reputation.

FILIPPO: I admit I spend too much but it's a habit now, and after all I have only one daughter. I've set aside money for her dowry and there's enough left to see me out. What surprises me is the threat to my family name you mention. What makes you say that, Fulgenzio?

FULGENZIO: I have good reason for it, especially since you have a daughter to marry. I know someone who would adore her as a wife and doesn't dare ask because you allow her to mingle indiscriminately with dapper young dandies—even invite them to travel with her.

FILIPPO: You mean Guglielmo?

FULGENZIO: I'm talking of the whole lot.

FILIPPO: Guglielmo is a sensible young man and honorable as the day is long.

FULGENZIO: Giacinta is young.

FILIPPO: My daughter is a good girl.

FULGENZIO: She's a woman.

FILIPPO: And my sister will be there.

FULGENZIO: Some old women are flightier than the young ones.

FILIPPO: I thought about that. Then I decided that so many people nowadays are doing the same thing . . .

FULGENZIO: Old friend, you've seen these things happen. And how have they all turned out? Happily?

FILIPPO: Some yes and some no.

FULGENZIO: Are you sure it will be yes with your daughter? Could it possibly be no?

FILIPPO: You're putting a flea in my ear. Tell me, who is this young man who wants to marry my daughter Giacinta?

FULGENZIO: I can't tell you right now.

FILIPPO: Why not?

FULGENZIO: Because at the moment he doesn't want his name mentioned. When things are different, he'll step forward himself.

FILIPPO: What am I supposed to do? Give up the country? That's impossible; I'm addicted to it.

FULGENZIO: Do you have to take your daughter along?

FILIPPO: If I didn't, there'd be the devil to pay.

FULGENZIO: Your daughter makes the decisions, does she?

FILIPPO: She always has.

FULGENZIO: Whose fault is that?

FILIPPO: Mine, I confess. It's my fault; I have a soft heart.

FULGENZIO: Soft heart or soft head? Fathers can spoil their daughters.

FILIPPO: What am I supposed to do?

FULGENZIO: Set the rules and make her abide by them. Get rid of the dandies who hang around.

FILIPPO: I wish I knew how to shake Guglielmo—in a nice way.

FULGENZIO: This Guglielmo will be her disgrace. It's because of him this other young man is staying away. He's a good match, if you're interested. Remember, there's nothing more monstrous than a girl ordering her father around.

FILIPPO: That's my fault, not hers.

FULGENZIO: Then it should be all the easier to get rid of Guglielmo.

FILIPPO: All the harder. I don't know how to go about it.

FULGENZIO: Are you a man or not?

FILIPPO: I'm no good at being blunt. Well, I'll just have to, somehow.

FULGENZIO: You'll be glad you did.

FILIPPO: Could you tell me who he is, this friend who wants to marry my daughter?

FULGENZIO: I'm sorry—for the moment I can't. Now I have to go. Forgive the liberty I've taken.

FILIPPO: I'm much obliged to you for it.

FULGENZIO: See you soon.

FILIPPO: Thank you for your honesty.

(Fulgenzio leaves, and Giacinta pokes her head in.)

GIACINTA: Has the old bore gone? Good.

FILIPPO: Call a servant for me.

GIACINTA: If you want the table set for dinner, I can tell them myself.

FILIPPO: No, I need someone for an errand.

GIACINTA: An errand where?

FILIPPO: You're too curious. It's my business.

GIACINTA: Something Signor Fulgenzio suggested?

FILIPPO: You take advantage of your old father.

GIACINTA: Who said so? Signor Fulgenzio?

FILIPPO: Mind your own affairs.

GIACINTA: Me? Your little girl? Your dear little Giacinta?

FILIPPO: Where are all the servants!

GIACINTA: Now, now, calm down. I'll call someone.

FILIPPO: Then hurry up.

GIACINTA: Aren't you going to tell me what you want a servant for?

FILIPPO: Damn it, I have a message for Guglielmo.

GIACINTA: Are you afraid he won't show up? He'll come—unfortunately.

FILIPPO: Why unfortunately? Didn't you say you wanted someone to talk to on the trip?

GIACINTA: You invited him. I didn't.

FILIPPO: Hmph.

GIACINTA: I'll call a servant. What shall he tell Guglielmo?

FILIPPO: Not to bother. We won't have room for him.

GIACINTA: (*Sarcastically.*) Oh, that will be charming!

FILIPPO: I'll put it politely.

GIACINTA: What reason can you possibly give him?

FILIPPO: I don't know. I'll say . . . your maid has to come along. She'll need his seat in the carriage.

GIACINTA: Better all the time!

FILIPPO: Are you making fun of me?

GIACINTA: What will he think? What will everybody say? Do you want to be called a boor?

FILIPPO: Do you think it looks proper to have a young man in your carriage?

GIACINTA: It's most improper. But think about it first. If I had invited him, you could say you didn't approve and get out of it. But you invited him yourself.

FILIPPO: Well, I made the mistake and I'll rectify it.

GIACINTA: You'll only make it worse. After all, if he is in the carriage with me, so are you and my aunt. It's not good, but it's not scandalous. But if you boot him out, everybody will know before the day is over. They'll say he and I were in love and you found out. They'll find fault with you and gossip about me. One innocent little act will leave our reputation in shreds.

FILIPPO: Maybe we should forget about the country.

GIACINTA: That might be better in one way, but in another, it would be worse. Imagine what they would say then! "Filippo is finished! He's out of money! His daughter, poor girl, is out of the picture now! Her dowry even is in doubt! Poor girl! Who will take her now? Who wants her? They have cut back on everything—on food, on entertaining. They put up a good front for awhile, but they're done for now." I can hear them.

FILIPPO: What should we do?

GIACINTA: Whatever you say.

FILIPPO: It's frying pan into the fire.

GIACINTA: Our reputation is at stake.

FILIPPO: Do you think it might be better if Guglielmo came with us?

GIACINTA: This time perhaps, since it's already done. But never again, mind you, never again. Stick to the rules of etiquette and never do it again. Well, shall I call a servant or not?

FILIPPO: Let it go. It's already done.

GIACINTA: That may be better. Let's go to dinner.

FILIPPO: Does he have to stay with us? At our villa?

GIACINTA: What did you actually say?

FILIPPO: Well, I invited him.

GIACINTA: Then how will you be able to get rid of him now?

FILIPPO: I suppose he'll have to stay with us.

GIACINTA: But never again, mind you, never again.

FILIPPO: Never, I promise you. Never, my dear little girl.

(He leaves as Brigida enters.)

BRIGIDA: A visitor to see you.

GIACINTA: At this hour? Who is it?

BRIGIDA: Signor Leonardo's sister Vittoria.

GIACINTA: Did you say I was in?

BRIGIDA: How could I say you were not?

GIACINTA: She certainly picked a fine time to come! Where is she?

BRIGIDA: She sent a servant ahead to say she's on her way here.

GIACINTA: Go meet her. See if she's going to the country or not and if there's any news. Coming at this hour, she must have some gossip to spread.

BRIGIDA: I heard something interesting.

GIACINTA: What?

BRIGIDA: I heard she had a new gown made and the tailor demanded to be paid before he'd give it to her. I heard there was a big row. She said if she didn't get the dress, she didn't want to go to the country. The story is all over town.

(Brigida goes and ushers in Vittoria.)

VITTORIA: Giacinta! My dearest!

GIACINTA: Vittoria, my precious!

(They kiss.)

VITTORIA: Isn't this a fine time to be bothering you?

GIACINTA: Bother me? When I heard you were coming, I was overjoyed.

VITTORIA: How are you? Feeling well?

GIACINTA: Wonderfully well. And you? No need to ask—you're fat and fresh, heaven bless you. Such a comfort.

VITTORIA: And you! You look adorable.

GIACINTA: How can you say that? I got up much too early; I didn't sleep; I have a stomach-ache and a head-ache. I can imagine how adorable I look.

VITTORIA: I don't know what's the matter with me; it's been days since I ate a thing, really nothing. I don't know what's keeping me alive. I must look like a stick.

GIACINTA: A stick? Those chubby little arms are hardly sticks.

VITTORIA: Well, I don't count any bones on you.

GIACINTA: No, thank heaven, I have enough flesh to keep me covered.

VITTORIA: Oh my dear Giacinta!

GIACINTA: Precious little Vittoria! (*They kiss.*) Sit down, my love. Go on, sit down.

VITTORIA: I did so want to see you. But you never come to see me.

(They sit.)

GIACINTA: Oh my dear, I never go anywhere. I just stay at home.

VITTORIA: I do too. I just stay at home and sit.

GIACINTA: I don't know how people can gad about town all day long.

(A small simpering pause.)

VITTORIA: Have you seen my brother recently?

GIACINTA: I saw him this morning.

VITTORIA: Tell me, what's the matter with him? He's so cross and fidgety.

GIACINTA: Well, we all have our bad days.

VITTORIA: I thought he might have quarreled with you.

GIACINTA: Quarreled with me? How could he? I respect him and admire him but I would never allow him to quarrel with me. Vittoria darling, will you stay and have dinner with us?

VITTORIA: Oh no, my precious, I can't. My brother is waiting for me.

GIACINTA: We'll send word to him.

VITTORIA: No, no, I really cannot.

GIACINTA: If you would favor us, we're about to sit down to dinner.

VITTORIA: You're dining so early?

GIACINTA: Yes, we're leaving for the country right away and we have to hurry. I must run off and change for the trip.

VITTORIA: (*Mortified.*) Yes—yes, of course. There'll be dust and you don't want to ruin your good dress.

GIACINTA: Oh, dust doesn't bother me. I'll put on something better than this old thing. I've had a duster made of silk and camel's hair, with it's own little hood, so there's no danger from dust. Don't you have a duster with a hood?

VITTORIA: Oh yes—yes, I still have mine from last year.

GIACINTA: Oh? I didn't see it on you last year.

VITTORIA: I didn't wear it because, if you remember, there was no dust last year.

GIACINTA: Oh yes. No dust last year.

VITTORIA: This year I had a dress made.

GIACINTA: Oh? I have a lovely one too.

VITTORIA: You'll see mine, and I'm sure you will approve.

GIACINTA: Mine is something special, as you'll see.

VITTORIA: In mine there's no flashy gold or silver but I have to tell you, it's stupendous!

GIACINTA: Oh, fashion! Fashion will be fashion!

VITTORIA: Well, no one can say mine is not in fashion.

GIACINTA: (*Laughing.*) Yes, I'm sure it is.

VITTORIA: You don't believe it?

GIACINTA: Of course I believe it.

VITTORIA: When it comes to fashion, I think I've always been among the first.

GIACINTA: What's this new dress of yours like?

VITTORIA: It's a *mariage.*

GIACINTA: A *mariage!*

VITTORIA: Yes, a *mariage.* I suppose you think that's not in fashion.

GIACINTA: How did you learn about the *mariage?*

VITTORIA: Probably the same way you did.

GIACINTA: Who made yours?

VITTORIA: The French tailor.

GIACINTA: Monsieur de la Réjouissance?

VITTORIA: Yes, Monsieur de la Réjouissance.

GIACINTA: The double-dealing traitor! He'll pay for that. I gave him all the details on how to make a *mariage.* I had Madame Granon's to work from.

VITTORIA: Madame Granon came to see me the day she arrived in Livorno.

GIACINTA: I don't care. That tailor will still have to answer to me.

VITTORIA: You're angry because I have a *mariage?*

GIACINTA: Darling! On the contrary, I'm delighted!

VITTORIA: Did you want to keep it all to yourself?

GIACINTA: Why? Do I look like an envious schoolgirl? I think you know I don't envy anyone. I leave others to do what they like. I pay no attention to what they're wearing. Every year I have a new dress. I expect prompt service and good service because I pay. I pay punctually and I don't make the tailor beg for his money.

VITTORIA: Everybody pays, I expect.

GIACINTA: No, they don't all pay. Some think that's old-fashioned. The latest fashion, they believe, is to keep the tailor waiting. They're not as well bred as you and I. Then when they run out of money, the tailor refuses to deliver. He wants his money first, and all kinds of nasty rows break out.

VITTORIA: Can you imagine!

GIACINTA: When are you going to wear your stupendous new dress?

VITTORIA: I haven't decided. I may not even put it on. That's the way I am. It's enough for me to have the old thing. I don't care about showing it off.

GIACINTA: If you were going to the country, that would be a wonderful opportunity to wear it. What a shame you're not going this year, you poor child!

VITTORIA: Who said I wasn't going?

GIACINTA: Oh, I don't know—didn't your brother Leonardo cancel the horses?

VITTORIA: Is that all? Can't all that be smoothed out any minute? Can't I go without him? Do you think I have no friends or relatives to turn to?

GIACINTA: Would you like to come with me?

VITTORIA: No, no, thank you so much.

GIACINTA: Really, I'd love to have you with us.

VITTORIA: I tell you what. If I can persuade a cousin of mine to go with me to Montenero, we may meet there.

GIACINTA: Oh, I'd adore that.

VITTORIA: When are you leaving?

GIACINTA: At two o'clock.

VITTORIA: Then I can stay a little while longer.

GIACINTA: Yes, yes, I see. (*Calling offstage.*) Wait a minute. I'll be right there.

VITTORIA: If you have things to do, please go ahead.

GIACINTA: Nothing important. They tell me dinner is ready and my father is eager to get started.

VITTORIA: Then I'll be on my way.

GIACINTA: No, no, if you want to stay, stay.

VITTORIA: I wouldn't want to upset your father.

GIACINTA: Frankly, he is a little touchy today.

VITTORIA: (*Rising.*) Then I'll get out of the way.

GIACINTA: (*Rising.*) Of course, if you'd like to stay, I'd be delighted. (*Calling off.*) I heard you. Can't you see I'm busy? Have some manners!

VITTORIA: Who is it you're talking to?

GIACINTA: They're hurrying me up. Some people are so rude.

VITTORIA: Yes, I know. But I didn't see anybody.

GIACINTA: Well, I did.

VITTORIA: I understand. Giacinta, until we meet again.

GIACINTA: Good-bye, dear. Remember me as I assure you I shall you.

VITTORIA: You can depend on it.

GIACINTA: One more little kiss.

VITTORIA: Yes, indeed, dear one.

GIACINTA: My precious.

(They kiss.)

VITTORIA: Good-bye.

GIACINTA: Good-bye.

VITTORIA: *(Muttering as she leaves.)* Insolent hussy! Being polite to her is killing me.

GIACINTA: Jealous brat! I can't stand envious women.

Scene 5

The room in Leonardo's house.
Leonardo and Fulgenzio.

LEONARDO: That's good news. So Signor Filippo promised to get out of taking Guglielmo along?

FULGENZIO: He gave me his word of honor.

LEONARDO: Will he keep it?

FULGENZIO: I'm sure he will. He has always dealt honorably with me.

LEONARDO: Then Guglielmo will not be going to the country with Giacinta.

FULGENZIO: There's not a chance.

LEONARDO: I'm very relieved. Now I'll gladly go.

FULGENZIO: I said enough and I did enough to open Filippo's eyes. He's very soft-hearted, and he may sometimes fall short out of sheer good nature, but he'll never fail you out of malice.

LEONARDO: His daughter winds him around her little finger.

FULGENZIO: Giacinta's not a bad girl. Filippo confessed she had nothing to do with inviting Guglielmo. He asked him himself to come with them because he likes company. He has a passion for extending hospitality.

LEONARDO: I'm glad Giacinta had no part in it. I thought it couldn't be so, after what had happened between her and me.

FULGENZIO: What did happen exactly?

LEONARDO: We just exchanged a few words. I assured her of my love, and I have reason to hope that she loves me.

FULGENZIO: Does her father know of this talk you had with her?

LEONARDO: Not from me.

FULGENZIO: No, I don't believe he does; because when I told him there was a suitor for his daughter, it never occurred to him to ask about you.

LEONARDO: I'm sure he isn't aware of it.

FULGENZIO: Well, he'll have to be told.

LEONARDO: Yes, some day.

FULGENZIO: Why not now?

LEONARDO: He's leaving for the country.

FULGENZIO: Friend, let's be frank with each other. I was glad to talk to Filippo for you and rid his daughter of a risky association because I believed it was the honest thing to do, and because you assured me your intentions toward her were honorable and once you were satisfied on this score you would ask her to marry you. Now I wouldn't want any more fancy dancing around, or I'll feel I've only made matters worse. You brought me into this, and I don't want any misunderstandings. One of two things: either you tell Filippo or I will.

LEONARDO: How do you think I should handle it?

FULGENZIO: Ask for her hand in marriage or else stop seeing her.

LEONARDO: How can I ask when time is so short?

FULGENZIO: It won't take long. I'll go to her father for you.

LEONARDO: Couldn't it wait till we're back from the country?

FULGENZIO: On vacation anything can happen. I know. I was young once. Thank heaven I didn't go completely crazy—but I had a few lapses. My obligation to my friend Filippo demands that I speak to him, either for you or against you.

LEONARDO: If that's how it is, then ask him for me. I must marry Giacinta.

FULGENZIO: Any conditions? What about dowry?

LEONARDO: I understand he's giving her eight thousand crowns and a trousseau.

FULGENZIO: Is that satisfactory?

LEONARDO: Oh very!

FULGENZIO: What about the wedding date?

LEONARDO: In four, six, eight months—whatever Signor Filippo says.

FULGENZIO: Very well, I'll talk to him.

LEONARDO: They're leaving today, remember.

FULGENZIO: Couldn't the trip be postponed a few days?

LEONARDO: Not a chance.

FULGENZIO: But this is important. It's worth waiting a little.

LEONARDO: If Signor Filippo stays, so will I. But you'll find it can't be done.

FULGENZIO: Why not?

LEONARDO: Because everybody is leaving. Signor Filippo will want to go, and Giacinta is determined to go today without fail, and my sister is tormenting the life out of me to go, and for a hundred other reasons I . . . can . . . not . . . stay!

FULGENZIO: Poh! this craze for the country has got completely out of hand. Business is forgotten! "Out of my way, I'm going this instant." But dear friend, allow me a heartfelt word or two. I know things are not going very well for you. Marry sensibly; don't put yourself deeper in debt. Eight thousand crowns can help a lot, but don't spend them on summer pleasures for your wife. Don't squander them in the country on vacationing. Prudence, economy, common sense. A quiet night's sleep, without palpitations and cold sweats, is worth more than all the pleasures in the world. While the money lasts, everyone has a wonderful time—at your expense. But when it's gone, all you will get is mockery and derision and "I told you so." Now excuse me. I'm off to talk with Signor Filippo. (*He leaves.*)

LEONARDO: (*Calling off.*) Hey! Anyone there?

(*Cecco appears.*)

CECCO: Did you call?

LEONARDO: Go to Signor Filippo's and tell him and his daughter that I am free now to join their party going to Montenero, and if they allow me I shall go with them. Hurry and bring me their answer. And tell Paolo I want him at once.

CECCO: Very well. (*He goes.*)

(*Leonardo feverishly begins to pack again.*)

(*Paolo enters.*)

PAOLO: You wanted me?

LEONARDO: Quick, get everything ready. And order the horses. We're leaving at two.

PAOLO: Oh, no!

LEONARDO: And hurry!

PAOLO: What about dinner?

LEONARDO: I don't care about dinner. Get ready to go.

PAOLO: But I unpacked everything.

LEONARDO: Pack again.

PAOLO: That's impossible.

LEONARDO: It has to be done! I want the coffee, the candles, the sugar, the chocolate . . .

PAOLO: I took it all back.

LEONARDO: Go get it again.

PAOLO: They won't let me have it.

LEONARDO: Don't make me angry.

PAOLO: But I tell you . . .

LEONARDO: Shut your mouth and do what I say. Hurry.

PAOLO: May I say something? Find somebody else. All this is more than I can handle.

LEONARDO: Now, Paolino, don't leave me in the lurch. After all these years of faithful service, don't walk out on me. Everything depends on this. I'll tell you something in confidence, as a friend. Here is the deal: Signor Filippo is giving me his daughter with a dowry of twelve thousand crowns. You want me to lose out now? You want me to be ruined? Don't you see I have to keep up a good front? Have you the heart to tell me you can't—it's impossible—you'll desert me?

PAOLO: I appreciate the trust you put in me. Very well, I'll do what I can, even if I have to dig into my savings. (*He goes.*)

LEONARDO: Good man!

(*He continues repacking his trunk.*)

(*Enter Vittoria, furious.*)

VITTORIA: I won't do it! I have never stayed in Livorno at this time of the year and I won't stay here now! I'm going to the country! Giacinta is going, everybody is going, and I am going too!

LEONARDO: You talk like a spoiled child.

VITTORIA: I'm not a child! I'll go with my cousin Lugrezia and her husband.

LEONARDO: Why not go with me?

VITTORIA: When?

LEONARDO: Today.

VITTORIA: Where?

LEONARDO: To the country.

VITTORIA: You?

LEONARDO: Yes, me.

VITTORIA: Oh!

LEONARDO: Yes! Word of honor!

VITTORIA: Are you fooling me?

LEONARDO: It's the truth.

VITTORIA: Truly truly?

LEONARDO: Don't you see I'm packing?

VITTORIA: Oh, my big old brother! What happened?

LEONARDO: It was this way: Signor Fulgenzio . . .

VITTORIA: Tell me about it later. Quick! Where are they? Where are the boxes? The linens! The mantles! The dresses! Where is my *mariage?*

(She runs out as Cecco enters.)

LEONARDO: Well? What did they say?

CECCO: I found the father and daughter together. They send their regards and they'll be delighted to have your company but they're sorry about the seat in their carriage because it's already been given to Signor Guglielmo.

LEONARDO: Guglielmo?

CECCO: That's what they said.

LEONARDO: Are you sure you heard correctly? Guglielmo?

CECCO: They've given it to Signor Guglielmo.

LEONARDO: No! It can't be! You're deaf! You're half-witted!

CECCO: I heard them all right, and I understood them too. Perfectly. If you need some proof, when I was leaving—just as I was going down the steps—I saw Signor Guglielmo and his servant arriving with all his luggage.

LEONARDO: What are they doing to me? They're making a fool of me! Fulgenzio has let me down! I'm a fool! I'm a fool! I'm a fool! (*He sits. Cecco starts out, very quietly.*) Bring me some water.

CECCO: To wash your hands?

LEONARDO: A glass of water, damn you!

(*He rises.*)

CECCO: Right away. (*He goes.*)

LEONARDO: (*Muttering to himself.*) I'm a fool. I'm a stupid ass. (*Cecco enters with a glass of water.*) Ass . . . ass . . . ass . . .

CECCO: Why?

LEONARDO: (*Taking the water.*) An ass, I tell you!

CECCO: (*His feelings hurt.*) I am not. I'm not an ass.

LEONARDO: I am! I'm an ass! I'm an ass!

(*He drinks the water.*)

CECCO: Asses do drink water. I drink wine.

LEONARDO: Go to Signor Fulgenzio's. See if he's home yet. Ask him to come here, or tell him I'll go to him.

CECCO: You'll go to Signor Fulgenzio's?

LEONARDO: Yes, you ass, where else?

CECCO: Are you talking to me?

LEONARDO: Yes, you ass, to you!

CECCO: Now we're both asses. (*He goes.*)

(*Paolo enters.*)

PAOLO: Good news! Everything will be ready to go.

LEONARDO: Leave me alone.

PAOLO: What's the matter? I did everything you asked me.

LEONARDO: Leave me alone, I tell you.

PAOLO: Has something gone wrong?

LEONARDO: Yes! Yes! Yes!

PAOLO: The horses are ordered.

LEONARDO: Cancel them.

PAOLO: Again?

LEONARDO: Oh, damn the luck!

PAOLO: What happened?

LEONARDO: Just leave me alone!

(*Vittoria enters with a dress folded over her arm.*)

VITTORIA: Want to see my *mariage?*

LEONARDO: Go away!

VITTORIA: Do you call that manners? Do you call that polite?

PAOLO: (*Quietly to Vittoria.*) Let him be.

VITTORIA: (*To Leonardo.*) What the devil is wrong with you?

LEONARDO: Go away!

VITTORIA: Do we have to put up with this all the way to the country? Can't you show a happy face for once?

LEONARDO: There'll be no more country, no more vacation, no more anything!

VITTORIA: You're not going to the country?

LEONARDO: No, and neither are you.

VITTORIA: Have you gone crazy?

PAOLO: (*To Vittoria.*) Don't upset him, for the love of heaven.

VITTORIA: (*To Paolo.*) Don't you tell me what to do!

(*Cecco returns.*)

CECCO: (*To Leonardo.*) Signor Fulgenzio is not at home.

LEONARDO: Where the devil has he gone?

CECCO: They told me he was at Signor Filippo's.

LEONARDO: (*To Paolo.*) Bring me my hat and sword.

PAOLO: Now don't do anything foolish.

LEONARDO: (*Interrupting.*) Bring me my hat and sword!

PAOLO: Very well. (*He goes.*)

VITTORIA: What are you going to do?

(*Leonardo doesn't answer.*)

(*Paolo returns with hat and sword.*)

LEONARDO: Give me my hat and sword.

PAOLO: Here you are.

VITTORIA: (*To Leonardo.*) What's wrong with you?

LEONARDO: You'll find out soon enough. (*He leaves.*)

VITTORIA: (*To Paolo.*) What's the matter with him?

PAOLO: I have no idea. I'll follow him. (*He leaves.*)

VITTORIA: (*To Cecco.*) Do you know what it could be?

CECCO: He said he was an ass and I was an ass, that's all I know. (*He leaves.*)

Scene 6

The room in Filippo's house.
Filippo and Fulgenzio.

FILIPPO: For myself I can tell you I'm very willing. Leonardo is a good boy, well brought up, and he has some property of his own. It's true that he likes to spend a bit, especially in the country, but he'll straighten out.

FULGENZIO: You're not the one to fault him for that.

FILIPPO: You mean I do the same? But there's a difference between him and me.

FULGENZIO: I'll say no more. You know him and you know your own circumstances. Let him have her, if you're so inclined; if you're not, let it pass.

FILIPPO: I'll gladly consent if that's what Giacinta wants.

FULGENZIO: I don't think she'll object.

FILIPPO: You know something?

FULGENZIO: A little more than you do. And I know things you ought to be more aware of than I. A father ought to keep his eyes open, especially with an only daughter. Girls shouldn't see too much of a young man. You understand? They shouldn't mix too freely. Didn't I tell you she's a woman? "Oh now," you said, "she's a good girl." And I said to you: "She's a *woman.*" With all her proper upbringing, with all her good-girlishness, there has been a little flirtation between her and Leonardo.

FILIPPO: Oh? A flirtation?

FULGENZIO: Yes, and you can thank heaven Leonardo is a gentleman. You'd better let him have her.

FILIPPO: Let him have her? He has to take her now, and she has to say yes. The little baggage! Flirtation, eh?

FULGENZIO: What do you think—girls are made of stucco? When you let them mingle too freely . . .

FILIPPO: Is Leonardo on his way here?

FULGENZIO: No, but I'll fetch him here so we can get this business signed and sealed.

FILIPPO: Once again I'm grateful to you.

FULGENZIO: Wasn't I right about separating Guglielmo from your daughter? Leonardo didn't understand how you could invite such a man to the country with you. If you had gone through with it, Leonardo was certainly not going to take her. Make sure Guglielmo doesn't see your daughter any more. You talk to her while I go get Leonardo.

FILIPPO: All right, if you say so, but we'll have to see . . .

FULGENZIO: Is there a problem?

FILIPPO: No . . . no . . .

FULGENZIO: I'll be right back then.

(He is about to leave when Guglielmo enters.)

GUGLIELMO: It's almost two o'clock. Shall I go get the horses?

FULGENZIO: What's this? Guglielmo?

FILIPPO: (*To Guglielmo.*) There's no hurry. We're not leaving for awhile. I have some things to do first.

FULGENZIO: You're off to the country, Guglielmo?

GUGLIELMO: Yes, I'm happy to say.

FULGENZIO: How are you traveling, may I ask?

GUGLIELMO: With Signor Filippo.

FULGENZIO: In his carriage?

GUGLIELMO: That's right.

FULGENZIO: With Giacinta?

GUGLIELMO: Yes.

FILIPPO: (*To Guglielmo.*) Oh, go fetch the horses.

GUGLIELMO: You said there was no hurry.

FILIPPO: Oh, run along, will you!

GUGLIELMO: I don't understand.

FILIPPO: Make sure the horses get their oats. Be good enough to stay there while they eat. Don't let the hostlers take their oats away from them.

GUGLIELMO: Their oats?

FILIPPO: Yes! Go now! Go!

GUGLIELMO: Yes . . . all right . . . I'm going. (*He leaves.*)

FILIPPO: Well, he's gone.

FULGENZIO: Nice work, Filippo.

FILIPPO: Well, when you give somebody your word . . .

FULGENZIO: Yes. You gave *me* your word. And this is how you keep it.

FILIPPO: Yes, but I gave *him* my word first.

FULGENZIO: If you wanted to keep your word to him, why did you promise me?

FILIPPO: Because I expected to do what you said.

FULGENZIO: Then why didn't you?

FILIPPO: Because . . . it would only go from bad to worse. Frying pan into the fire! Because people would have said—they would have . . . ! Oh, if you had heard all the reasons my daughter trotted out, you'd understand. You'd be convinced yourself. You'd see why!

FULGENZIO: Oh, I understand. I see I'm not dealing with gentlemen here. I'll explain as best I can to Leonardo. I'm sorry I ever got mixed up in this. I won't make the same mistake again.

(He is about to leave.)

FILIPPO: No, listen!

FULGENZIO: I don't want to hear any more.

FILIPPO: Listen to me for just a minute.

FULGENZIO: What can you possibly say now?

FILIPPO: Old friend, I'm so confused I don't know where I am.

FULGENZIO: Bad business, bad business.

FILIPPO: Help me find a way out.

FULGENZIO: How?

FILIPPO: Couldn't we still get rid of Guglielmo?

FULGENZIO: You sent him to get your horses!

FILIPPO: I didn't want him around. What else could I do?

FULGENZIO: What happens when he comes back?

FILIPPO: I don't know. I'm confused. Have you got any ideas?

FULGENZIO: Better give up going to the country.

FILIPPO: How can I do that?

FULGENZIO: Take sick. Say you don't feel well.

FILIPPO: Sick with what?

FULGENZIO: (*Irritated.*) Try leprosy.

FILIPPO: Don't get angry now.

(Leonardo enters.)

LEONARDO: Here you are! Both of you! Which one of you is making a fool of me? Which one? Who did this to me?

FULGENZIO: (*To Filippo.*) Answer him.

FILIPPO: (*To Fulgenzio.*) Old friend, you tell him.

LEONARDO: Is this the way for a gentleman to behave? What kind of low-down uncivil behavior is this?

FULGENZIO: (*To Filippo.*) Answer him.

FILIPPO: (*To Fulgenzio.*) I can't think of a thing to say!

(Giacinta enters.)

GIACINTA: What's all the shouting? What are you brawling about?

LEONARDO: I'm not brawling. It's the tricksters and the cheats that betray people who put faith in their word of honor.

GIACINTA: Who? Who's a cheat? Who's a trickster?

FULGENZIO: (*To Filippo.*) You tell her. Speak up.

FILIPPO: (*To Fulgenzio.*) You first.

FULGENZIO: All right, since I'm now entangled in this mess and Filippo won't speak, I will. Yes, my girl, Leonardo has every right to complain. After assuring him that Guglielmo would not be coming with you, to go back on your word and bring him along anyhow, to take him in your carriage to the country is hardly defensible. Leonardo is right: it's downright uncivil.

GIACINTA: What do you say, father?

FILIPPO: He's talking to you. You answer him.

GIACINTA: Be good enough to tell me, Signor Fulgenzio, what authority does Signor Leonardo have to order other people around?

LEONARDO: The authority that any decent . . .

GIACINTA: (*Interrupting after the first word.*) Excuse me, but I'm talking to Signor Fulgenzio. How dare Signor Leonardo presume to decide whom my father and I may see, whom we may invite to the country with us?

LEONARDO: You know very well . . .

GIACINTA: (*Interrupting again.*) I am not addressing you. Let Signor Fulgenzio answer me.

FILIPPO: (*To Fulgenzio.*) I wouldn't call this flirtation.

FULGENZIO: (*To Giacinta.*) Since you want an answer from me, I'll tell you. Leonardo wouldn't say a word—he wouldn't presume anything at all if he didn't intend to marry you.

GIACINTA: (*To Fulgenzio.*) Signor Leonardo intends to marry me?

LEONARDO: It's news to you perhaps?

GIACINTA: (*To Leonardo.*) Please allow me to speak with Signor Fulgenzio —without interruption, if you will be so kind. (*To Fulgenzio.*) Tell us what basis you have for such a statement.

FULGENZIO: Basis? Well, I myself was commissioned by Leonardo to present a proposal to your father, which I did. That's the basis.

LEONARDO: But seeing how I've been mistreated . . .

GIACINTA: (*To Leonardo.*) Be quiet, please, and wait for your turn. I'll get around to you. (*Distantly, to the room at large.*) What did my father say to this proposal?

FILIPPO: What would *you* say to it?

GIACINTA: First tell me what you think. Then I'll tell you what I think.

FILIPPO: Well . . . I say . . . as far as I'm concerned . . . there's no problem.

LEONARDO: But as things now stand, I am not . . .

GIACINTA: It's not your turn yet. It's my turn. Be good enough to listen to me carefully, and then you can answer if you like. Ever since I have known Signor Leonardo, he cannot deny that I have shown him respect; and I know that he has respected me. Little by little respect develops into liking; and I believe he loves me just as I confess I am not indifferent to Signor Leonardo. However, in order for a man to establish any rights with a young woman, a secret passion is not enough—there must be an open declaration. Even then it is not enough for the girl to know it. The parents must know it too. The whole world must be informed. The relationship must be established with due formality. After that is done, then a man deserves every deference and courtesy; then he has the right to state his wishes—but not his demands. Because a decent girl can still see anyone she likes and talk to anyone as an equal. Of course she must not show preference for others or attract attention or misbehave. With the same modesty I always showed toward you, I also behaved with Guglielmo. My father invited him to join us and I was quite content—as I would have been with anyone else; and you are wrong when you complain about him and me. Now that you have declared your intentions, now that you publicly express your love and do me the honor of asking for my hand in marriage—and my father consents—I can tell you that I am willing to accept your devotion, and I thank you for your kind offer. In the future I shall defer to you, as I should. You may speak, and you will be heard. I ask only one small favor, and on that favor may depend my good opinion of you and my satisfaction with this arrangement. You want me to love you, but I'm sure you don't expect me to be discourteous to others. Don't let the first tokens of your love be suspicion and boorish behavior. We're about to leave for the country. Do you want us departing under a gloomy cloud of your suspicions, making us all uncomfortable with one another? Leave things as they are for awhile. Have faith in me and don't insult me with your suspicions. I shall know from that if you really love me—if it is my heart you want, or my hand. My hand is ready, if you want it. But my heart you'll have to earn, if that is what you truly desire.

FILIPPO: (*To Fulgenzio.*) What do you say to that?

FULGENZIO: (*Quietly.*) I wouldn't take her for a hundred thousand crowns.

LEONARDO: I don't know what to say. I love you. I want your love above all things. You have given me reasons that win me over completely. I don't want to be ungrateful. Do as you like, and have pity on me.

FULGENZIO: Ooo! The fool!

(Brigida enters.)

BRIGIDA: Signor Leonardo, your sister is here with your manservant.

LEONARDO: (*To Filippo.*) With your permission, let her come in.

BRIGIDA: (*Softly to Giacinta.*) Are we going or not?

GIACINTA: (*Softly to Brigida.*) We're going, we're going.

BRIGIDA: I was afraid we wouldn't.

(Vittoria comes in looking depressed, followed by Paolo.)

VITTORIA: May I come in?

GIACINTA: Oh yes, my precious, come in!

VITTORIA: (*Muttering.*) Precious! (*To her brother.*) How are you feeling, Leonardo? Are you all right?

LEONARDO: I'm fine, thank heaven. Paolino—quick, get everything ready

—the trunk, the horses, all the supplies. We're leaving right away.

VITTORIA: (*Brightening.*) We're leaving?

GIACINTA: Yes, we're leaving. Aren't you glad?

VITTORIA: Yes, my precious, I'm very glad.

FILIPPO: (*To Fulgenzio.*) I like to see sisters-in-law so friendly.

FULGENZIO: Like the fox and the hen.

FILIPPO: You're a strange man.

PAOLO: Heaven be praised! Blue skies again! (*He leaves.*)

VITTORIA: Come, brother! Let's go, let's go!

LEONARDO: You're very impatient.

GIACINTA: The poor girl is impatient to get to the country.

VITTORIA: Yes, just as you are.

FULGENZIO: You're leaving without drawing up the contract?

VITTORIA: What contract?

FILIPPO: Yes, we should really put it in writing before we go.

VITTORIA: Put what in writing?

LEONARDO: I'm more than willing.

VITTORIA: To do what?

GIACINTA: We need two witnesses.

VITTORIA: Witnesses for what?

BRIGIDA: (*To Vittoria.*) Don't you know?

VITTORIA: I don't know anything!

BRIGIDA: You will soon enough.

VITTORIA: Leonardo . . .

LEONARDO: What?

VITTORIA: . . . are you getting married?

LEONARDO: M-hm.

VITTORIA: And you didn't say a word about it to me?

LEONARDO: Give me time.

VITTORIA: And this is your wife?

GIACINTA: Yes, dear, I'm the lucky girl. Do you wish me well?

VITTORIA: Oh, I'm delighted! You don't know how happy that makes me! My dear sister-in-law! And my dear brother, taking a wife before he finds a husband for me. I'll talk to you about that later, Leonardo.

FILIPPO: (*To Fulgenzio.*) You see how well they get along?

FULGENZIO: (*To Filippo.*) Oh, I see all right. You just don't know women.

(*Guglielmo and Ferdinando enter.*)

GIACINTA: Here they are. Here are our two witnesses.

GUGLIELMO: The horses are ready.

FERDINANDO: Come along, come along, it's late. How is friend Leonardo? Still in the dumps?

LEONARDO: What do you mean—in the dumps?

FERDINANDO: Oh, something Vittoria said.

VITTORIA: No, I didn't. I never said a word.

FERDINANDO: You've forgotten. It's a woman's prerogative.

FILIPPO: Gentlemen, before we leave there's something I must tell you. Leonardo has been good enough to ask me for my daughter, and I have consented. We'll be having a wedding. (*To Leonardo.*) When shall it be?

LEONARDO: I'd say right after we return.

FILIPPO: Very well, we'll have the wedding ceremony after we return. Meanwhile we must draw up the contract. I ask you two to be witnesses.

GUGLIELMO: This is unexpected news.

FERDINANDO: I'm ready and willing. Let's do the needful and get on the road. By the way, where do I sit?

FILIPPO: I wouldn't know . . . What do you say, Giacinta?

GIACINTA: That's up to you.

FILIPPO: And where's a seat for Guglielmo? How do we manage this?

VITTORIA: (*To Filippo.*) Allow me to suggest something.

FERDINANDO: Yes, you solve the problem for us.

VITTORIA: Since my brother is promised to Giacinta, he should ride in the carriage with his bride-to-be.

FULGENZIO: Yes, that would be proper, Filippo.

FILIPPO: Giacinta? What do you say?

GIACINTA: I'm neutral: I invite no one; I refuse no one.

LEONARDO: What do you say, Guglielmo?

GUGLIELMO: I say that I am one too many. I shall stay behind.

VITTORIA: No, no, you'll come in the carriage with me.

GUGLIELMO: If Signor Leonardo permits, I shall accept your kind invitation.

LEONARDO: (*Nonplussed.*) Yes, of course. I shall be much obliged.

FILIPPO: (*To Fulgenzio.*) Now what do you say? Everything's going to be smooth sailing.

FULGENZIO: (*To Filippo.*) Not for Vittoria.

FERDINANDO: And where do I fit in?

GIACINTA: You can go with my maid, if you don't mind.

FERDINANDO: In the little buggy?

GIACINTA: In the two-seater, yes.

FERDINANDO: (*To Brigida.*) So—joy of my life, I shall have the pleasure of your delightful company.

BRIGIDA: Oh, I'm overwhelmed. The excitement may be too much for me.

FERDINANDO: I'm sure you'd rather have Leonardo's manservant.

FULGENZIO: Good, good! Everybody's happy. Harmony reigns supreme.

VITTORIA: Come on, what are we waiting for? Let's get to this blessed country.

GIACINTA: Yes, let's sign the contract and be off. The great moment has finally arrived . . . after all our wishing and waiting and agonizing for fear we'd never go. All the usual frenzy of the season. So, a happy journey to those about to depart and a happy stay for those who remain at home.

Villeggiatura

Part Two: Adventures in the Country

Continuing Characters from CRAZY FOR THE COUNTRY

LEONARDO
PAOLO
VITTORIA
FERDINANDO
FILIPPO
GUGLIELMO
GIACINTA
BRIGIDA

New Characters of ADVENTURES IN THE COUNTRY

(*in order of speaking*)

TITA
manservant to Costanza and waiter at the coffee shop

BELTRAME
manservant to Tognino's father and waiter at the coffee shop

A SERVANT TO FILIPPO

SABINA
an aged aunt of Giacinta

COSTANZA

ROSINA
her niece

TOGNINO
a foolish youngster in love with Rosina

TIME: *Early autumn, 1761.*
PLACE: *The countryside of Montenero, near Livorno.*

Scene 1

A ground-floor salon in Filippo's villa. Morning. There are card tables and chairs, a loveseat, etc. Large doors at the rear opening on the garden.

Brigida brings in three other servants—Paolino, Tita, and Beltrame— from the kitchen.

BRIGIDA: Come on in. They are all still asleep.

PAOLINO: At our place they just went to bed.

TITA: Ours too. They won't wake up till noon.

BELTRAME: When they're up all night, they have to get some sleep during the day.

PAOLINO: How about you, Brigida? How did you manage to get up so early?

BRIGIDA: Oh, I had a good night's sleep. As soon as they started their card games I went to bed. They played, they had some supper, they played some more—and I slept through it all. At daybreak the mistress called for me and I helped her undress, put her to bed, closed the door, and dressed for the day. I had a little walk in the orchard, picked some jasmines in the garden, and just enjoyed the peace and quiet.

PAOLINO: It's really the best time of the day. And they never see it.

BRIGIDA: City and country are alike to them. They lead the same life everywhere.

PAOLINO: No difference . . . except they see more people in the country . . . and spend more money.

BRIGIDA: (*Brightly.*) Well now, this morning I want to have the honor of treating my three cavaliers. What will you have? Coffee, chocolate, something stronger? You name it.

PAOLINO: Chocolate for me.

TITA: For me too.

BELTRAME: I'll have a glass of the good stuff.

BRIGIDA: Coming right up. (*She is about to go to the kitchen.*)

TITA: (*To Brigida, hinting broadly.*) I never take chocolate without something on the side.

BRIGIDA: Of course. I hear you.

PAOLINO: Brigida knows how to do things.

BRIGIDA: The cupboards are still full but they won't be for long, so we'd better enjoy some of it while we can. (*She goes to the kitchen.*)

PAOLINO: Tomorrow morning I'll expect you all at my place.

TITA: Good. And the next morning is on me.

PAOLINO: (*To Tita.*) Is your master in the country too?

TITA: No, he's sweltering in Livorno, while the mistress is here enjoying herself. He wears himself out working in the city and she spends his money on a good time in the country.

PAOLINO: Your Signora Costanza certainly cuts a fine figure here. Nobody would guess she's a shopkeeper's wife.

BELTRAME: Yes, we call her the Countess of Montenero.

PAOLINO: Who is the girl staying with her this year?

TITA: Her niece, poor little thing. And I mean poor! Every rag on her back is a gift from my mistress.

PAOLINO: Why does Signora Costanza put that extra burden on her husband? Why bring a niece to the country and pay for her clothes besides?

TITA: I'll tell you why. Signora Costanza is still young enough herself; but here in Montenero there are some even younger than she is. And where the young things are, other young things gather around; so to attract a little of that young blood, she brings along a niece just sixteen years old.

(Brigida and another Servant bring in chocolate, wine, etc. The Servant returns to the kitchen.)

BRIGIDA: Here we are . . . here we are. Sorry if I have kept you waiting.

PAOLINO: Not at all. We've been having a good time.

BRIGIDA: Doing what?

PAOLINO: (*Laughing.*) Talking about the neighbors.

BRIGIDA: Good. Books could be written about what goes on during country vacations. Come to the country if you want material for a comedy. Paolino, your chocolate. (*Giving Paolino a cup.*) Look at our old lady, for instance. Here's yours, Tita. (*Giving Tita a cup.*) She's seventy-five years old and still expecting to be courted. (*Giving both men little biscuits.*) Signor Ferdinando knows how to get around her by pretending to be smitten dead by her charms—and the old biddy falls for it! I think he's plucking her pinfeathers. (*She pours wine into a glass and gives it to Beltrame.*) Beltrame, this should please you.

BELTRAME: (*Chuckling.*) The best chocolate in the world.

BRIGIDA: Have some biscuits. What's this they're saying about Signor Guglielmo being in love with your mistress Vittoria? Is it true, Paolino? You must know all about it.

PAOLINO: I hear something went on between them in the carriage during the drive from Livorno. The groom, who sat behind, says the little carriage window was open and they shut it, but he could still hear things from time to time.

BRIGIDA: Ooo! Two young people in a carriage . . . it's the chance of a lifetime.

BELTRAME: (*Handing back his glass.*) Good, very good.

BRIGIDA: Would you like another?

BELTRAME: No, that's fine.

BRIGIDA: Go on, have one more.

BELTRAME: No, really.

BRIGIDA: One more—for me.

BELTRAME: For you? Give it here. I'd do more that that—for you.

BRIGIDA: I like men . . .

BELTRAME: Eh?

BRIGIDA: I like men who try a little harder.

PAOLINO: Tomorrow—Brigida, Tita, Beltrame—I'll expect you all at my place.

TITA: And the day after tomorrow at mine.

BELTRAME: I'm sorry I can't invite you to my place. My master never drinks coffee or chocolate at home, so we never get a whiff.

PAOLINO: Your master is the doctor here in Montenero, isn't he?

BELTRAME: Yes, he's been here for years.

PAOLINO: Yesterday morning he was at our house drinking chocolate.

BRIGIDA: He was? He had some here too.

TITA: What if I told you he had chocolate at our place too?

BRIGIDA: Good for the doctor! He gets around.

PAOLINO: He'll probably make the rounds again this morning.

BELTRAME: Not today. He's in Maremma and won't be back till tomorrow.

BRIGIDA: How come you didn't go with him?

BELTRAME: He left us here to look after his son.

BRIGIDA: That fool Tognino?

TITA: Fool is right! That boy is a real numbskull. He's making calf love to Rosina.

BRIGIDA: Signora Costanza's niece?

BELTRAME: That's right. While the doctor practices on Signora Costanza, the son apprentices on the niece.

BRIGIDA: Really! Tell me about it.

(Noises off.)

PAOLINO: People are coming.

TITA: Let's get out of here.

BRIGIDA: We'll go through the garden. I want to hear all about it.

PAOLINO: *(Leaving.)* Fine doings.

TITA: *(Leaving.)* Just the usual fooling around.

BELTRAME: The fruits of youth!

BRIGIDA: That's what we come to the country for.

(They go laughing into the garden.)

(Ferdinando enters in a robe.)

FERDINANDO: Hey! Anyone there? Everybody still asleep? Hey! Who's there? Hey! Hey!

(The Servant comes in.)

SERVANT: You wanted something?

FERDINANDO: What the devil! You have to yell yourself hoarse to get some service here.

SERVANT: Sorry.

FERDINANDO: Bring me some chocolate.

SERVANT: Very well.

(Ferdinando sits at one of the card tables and takes a little notebook out of his pocket. He reads from it and makes notations.)

FERDINANDO: Won at minchiate, eighteen lire. Won at primiera, seventy-two lire. Won at ventuno, ninety-six lire. At faro, won sixteen. That makes . . . *(Counting it up.)* two hundred two. Not bad. *(Shouting.)* Where the devil's my chocolate? Are you ever coming with the chocolate I asked for, you blasted . . .

(Filippo enters.)

FILIPPO: My dear friend! Please don't shout.

FERDINANDO: Your servants do as they please and you don't say a word.

FILIPPO: They serve me very well and I never have to shout.

FERDINANDO: I'm not thinking about myself. But your other guests are complaining about the service.

FILIPPO: Let me tell you, friend—I pay my servants myself, and whoever is not happy is free to go elsewhere.

FERDINANDO: Have you had your chocolate yet?

FILIPPO: No.

FERDINANDO: Why not?

FILIPPO: I'm waiting till I'm ready for it.

FERDINANDO: I'd like to have some now.

FILIPPO: Go ahead.

FERDINANDO: I ordered it three hours ago. (*Bawling into the wings.*) Hey! Am I ever going to get that chocolate?

FILIPPO: Don't yell.

FERDINANDO: But they don't bring it!

FILIPPO: Be patient. They're busier than usual, and they can't do everything at once. We're giving a dinner today and they're getting everything ready.

FERDINANDO: I wouldn't count on it. Your servant, Signor Filippo.

FILIPPO: Where are you going?

FERDINANDO: To get my chocolate somewhere else.

FILIPPO: Dear friend, between you and me, you sin a little on the side of gluttony.

FERDINANDO: My stomach is weak. I eat practically nothing at night.

FILIPPO: At Leonardo's supper yesterday evening you did very well by everything on the table.

FERDINANDO: Yesterday was an exception.

FILIPPO: If I had consumed what you did, I couldn't eat for three days.

(*The servant brings a cup on a tray.*)

FERDINANDO: Here's my chocolate.

FILIPPO: I thought you were going out for yours. You go right ahead. I'll drink this.

FERDINANDO: Have I upset you?

FILIPPO: No, I don't get upset about such things. You run on along. I'll take this.

FERDINANDO: You're just being kind. I don't want you to be upset. I'll drink it.

(*He takes the cup from the tray.*)

FILIPPO: Such ceremony! I hate to see you force yourself. (*To the Servant.*) Whip up a cup of chocolate for me too.

SERVANT: I'm afraid there isn't any more.

FILIPPO: Didn't you steep some last night as usual?

SERVANT: Yes, but it's all gone now.

FILIPPO: My daughter didn't drink it, my sister didn't drink it—so where did the chocolate go?

SERVANT: I really don't know, but there is none left.

FILIPPO: Well, if it's all gone, I'll have to do without. But then I'm used to that.

(*The Servant bows and goes out.*)

FERDINANDO: It's good. Your chocolate is really very good.

FILIPPO: I'm glad. I'll try to get you a larger supply.

FERDINANDO: Now, with your permission, I'll dress for my morning walk.

FILIPPO: Come, let's play a hand or two of picchetto first.

FERDINANDO: At this hour?

FILIPPO: Yes, while no one's around. If I wait till later, they choose their partners and leave me out.

FERDINANDO: My dear Signor Filippo, I don't feel like playing now.

FILIPPO: A couple of hands. Please.

FERDINANDO: Excuse me, it's time for my walk. Later, later . . . we'll play a game later. (*He leaves.*)

(*Filippo sits alone at the table and sets out cards for a game of solitaire.*)

(*Giacinta drifts in. Filippo sees her, scraps his solitaire spread, and rises from his chair. Giacinta shakes her head at his gesture inviting her to sit down and join him. She continues up to the garden doors, where she looks out.*)

(*Filippo drops the cards on the table and goes out, looking very dispirited.*)

(*Brigida runs in from the garden, some flowers in hand. She offers them to Giacinta, who turns away.*)

BRIGIDA: Why are you so melancholy? This year you seem to take no pleasure in the country.

GIACINTA: I curse the day we came here.

BRIGIDA: But why?

GIACINTA: Don't ask.

BRIGIDA: If I knew what it was, perhaps I could help.

GIACINTA: Brigida, I know I've been acting strange. I'm going crazy. My sins are catching up with me.

BRIGIDA: What sins? You mean promising to marry Signor Leonardo?

GIACINTA: No, I don't regret that. Leonardo has his good points. He loves me tenderly, and he'll never mistreat me. No, what I regret—bitterly regret—is insisting on having Guglielmo travel with us, and letting my father lodge him in our house.

BRIGIDA: Does Signor Leonardo object?

GIACINTA: Leave Leonardo out of it. He has suffered enough—and all because of me.

BRIGIDA: What has Signor Guglielmo done? He seems such an honest and civil young gentleman.

GIACINTA: That's just it. He's so polite, so courteous. That soothing, persuasive way of his, so sweet, so touching, so winning—he has charmed me. Yes, I'm in love—as much in love as a woman can be.

BRIGIDA: How did it happen? You told me so many times you never thought about him.

GIACINTA: I know. And it's true; I never gave him a thought. He didn't mean a thing to me. I used to laugh to myself at the attentions he wasted on me. But oh Brigida!—being together, seeing him every day at all hours—that unfailing courtesy of his, always finding the right words at the right time—and then sitting beside him at the table, feeling him brush against me now and then—whether by accident or not—and then asking my pardon, and sighing—these things are fatal! They're horribly insidious, and I don't know how, I don't know where they are going to end . . . or where I want them to end.

BRIGIDA: But it's not your fault. Your father invited him.

GIACINTA: Yes, that's true. I've been trying to put the blame on my father because he started the whole thing. Still, it was up to me to stop it. I was the only one who could, and it was my duty to put an end to the whole . . . the whole crazy affair!—But I didn't care! I liked having my own way. I enjoyed the power of making Guglielmo suffer, the power to inflict pain. I reveled in the wounded look in his eyes. So I let it go on . . . because I didn't care one way or the other. I accepted the whole impossible situation. Then acceptance became pleasure . . . and pleasure became passion.

BRIGIDA: Does Signor Leonardo suspect anything?

GIACINTA: I don't think so. I'm careful as I can be, but I swear I'm suffering the pangs of hell, having to show Leonardo the attentions I owe to him as my future husband . . . and at the same time, when I do, watching Guglielmo suffer, watching him wince, this man who has won my heart—all this has become a torment I cannot describe.

BRIGIDA: What are you going to do about it?

GIACINTA: I don't know, and that's what terrifies me. I don't trust myself.

BRIGIDA: After all, you're not married yet.

GIACINTA: Are you suggesting I go back on my word? I signed a marriage contract! I signed it! My father signed it! All the relatives know—on both sides. It's been published in town! What would people say? But there's worse. If they discover I love Guglielmo, won't they say I was indulging my passion for him while we were still in Livorno, that I arranged to have him with me here to carry on the affair, that I had the audacity to sign a marriage contract with another man—and brought Guglielmo to the country so I could live openly with him in the same house? My reputation is at stake. These are things I shudder to think about.

BRIGIDA: It's a pickle all right. I feel sorry for you, terribly sorry. But isn't everybody saying that Signor Guglielmo is in love with . . . someone else?

GIACINTA: With Vittoria? There's no truth in that. He pretends to be . . . as a cover to hide his feelings for me.

BRIGIDA: Then . . . Signor Guglielmo knows you favor him.

GIACINTA: I try to hide it, but he knows very well. And then that foolish aunt of mine, the old trouble-maker—she tumbled to it and instead of trying to stop it, she enjoys adding fuel to the fire. It's mostly my fault I'm so vulnerable and weak.

BRIGIDA: Speak of the devil—here she comes.

(Sabina enters and crosses up to the garden doors calling:)

SABINA: Ferdinando!

GIACINTA: She's in her second childhood. She makes a thousand crude remarks and tries to pass them off as jokes.

BRIGIDA: Tell her. Warn her not to give Signor Guglielmo false hopes.

GIACINTA: No, no, don't say a word to her! She'll only get worse.

BRIGIDA: M-hm. The sick won't take their medicine.

(Sabina crosses down to Giacinta.)

SABINA: Niece, have you seen Ferdinando?

GIACINTA: No, not this morning.

SABINA: How about you, Brigida? Have you seen Signor Ferdinando?

BRIGIDA: He was here earlier but he's gone out.

SABINA: Naughty boy. He told me last night he would have chocolate with me in my room this morning, and he's nowhere in sight. He's on the go all day long, calling on all kinds of people. Busy, busy, busy. Ungrateful boy.

BRIGIDA: You poor dear.

SABINA: (*To Giacinta.*) Have you had your chocolate?

GIACINTA: No, aunt.

SABINA: Why didn't you order some? We could have had a cozy cup together in my room.

GIACINTA: I didn't want any this morning.

SABINA: (*Smiling at her knowingly.*) Guglielmo was there. He came to my room, so I ordered chocolate for us both. Guglielmo whipped it into a fine froth with his own hands. You can see that young blade really knows how to stir things up! Creamy and delicious! Whatever that young buck lays a hand on, he does to a faretheewell!

BRIGIDA: You don't do so badly yourself.

SABINA: (*To Giacinta.*) What's the matter? Aren't you feeling well?

GIACINTA: I have a little headache.

SABINA: I don't know what young people are coming to! All you hear from them is their headaches and stomach-aches and swooning. Everybody's swooning. I wouldn't change places with one of you young girls for all the money in the world.

GIACINTA: Yes, you have a wonderful constitution.

BRIGIDA: Like a horse.

SABINA: At least I enjoy a good time. I don't come to the country to mope. Why isn't Ferdinando here? (*To Brigida.*) Call me somebody to look for him.

GIACINTA: Now, aunt, don't make yourself ridiculous before everybody.

SABINA: What do you mean—make myself ridiculous? I'm not allowed to show partiality for a person? I'm a widow, ain't I, and free to do as I like?

GIACINTA: Very true. But at your age . . .

SABINA: My age? My age? I'm not a sniveling child, if that's what you man. I'm in the bloom of womanhood and I know my way around better than you do.

GIACINTA: Aren't you ashamed to say such things?

SABINA: Ashamed? Why? A woman who is available, whether she's a widow or a girl, is permitted to have a suitor. But two at the same time is in bad taste. I believe you know what I mean.

GIACINTA: I marvel at the way you talk. Do what you please. I'll stay out of your affairs and I beg you to stay out of mine. (*She leaves.*)

SABINA: Brazen hussy! As if I didn't know her secrets!

BRIGIDA: Pardon my saying so, but that's not the way to help her. If you know something's amiss, you should try to stop it, or at least not shout it out before everybody. Reputations are at stake. Do you want to disgrace your niece? What's been has been, and there's no use blabbing about it and creating scandal and dissension in the family.

SABINA: You just stop blabbing and send for Signor Ferdinando.

(*Enter Ferdinando.*)

FERDINANDO: Here I am, here I am, at your service.

SABINA: (*Fuming.*) Where have you been?

FERDINANDO: At the druggist's. I had a little indigestion and he gave me some rhubarb for it.

SABINA: (*Softening.*) Poor dear. Are you better now?

FERDINANDO: Yes, I feel a little better.

SABINA: My poor sweet suffering boy! That's why you didn't come to my room for chocolate this morning.

FERDINANDO: I'm sorry about that. But I knew you would forgive me.

SABINA: (*To Brigida.*) Now you go away.

BRIGIDA: Oh, of course. I wouldn't think of interfering with your courting. (*She leaves.*)

SABINA: I don't care what anybody says as long as my Ferdinando loves me.

FERDINANDO: Right now I need time to digest my breakfast.

SABINA: Dear little Ferdinando.

FERDINANDO: Dear . . . Sabina.

SABINA: Get me a chair.

FERDINANDO: Of course. Gladly. (*He brings her a chair.*)

SABINA: (*Sitting.*) Why don't you sit down beside me?

FERDINANDO: I've been sitting all morning.

SABINA: Sit down, I tell you.

FERDINANDO: You tell me?

SABINA: Yes, you are mine to command, and I command you to sit down.

FERDINANDO: (*Taking a chair.*) Ours not to reason why.

SABINA: What an adorable boy! And how you adore me!

FERDINANDO: (*Sitting.*) Ours but to do or die.

SABINA: Come a little closer.

FERDINANDO: (*Barely edging in.*) Yes. Here I am.

SABINA: Closer than that.

FERDINANDO: There's rhubarb on my breath.

SABINA: You naughty boy! I'll come closer then. (*She does.*) My dearest little piggy, you must control yourself and not overdo. Last night you ate a tiny bit too much. No more of that. Today at dinner you'll sit next to me. I want to see you don't overeat again. You'll take just the portions I give you.

FERDINANDO: There's plenty of time before dinner. I'll be feeling fine by then and can enjoy a good meal.

SABINA: No. my precious, I want you to limit yourself.

FERDINANDO: What time is it?

SABINA: Here's my watch, you read it. Don't you have a watch?

FERDINANDO: I had one, but it was slow. I left it in Livorno.

SABINA: Why? A gentleman looks odd without a watch, especially in the country.

FERDINANDO: Yes, it's embarrassing. I feel ashamed, but what can I do? I'm almost ready to go back to Livorno for it.

SABINA: If my watch had a man's chain, I'd gladly lend it to you.

FERDINANDO: Chains are easy to find, even in Montenero.

SABINA: Yes, a chain could be found. But what would I do without my watch?

FERDINANDO: I see you didn't really mean to give it to me. You were only teasing me. I will go back to Livorno.

SABINA: No, no, dear, I did mean it. Take it, my precious, take it. But I'm lending it to you, you understand?

FERDINANDO: Naturally.

SABINA: You see how fond of you I am?

FERDINANDO: Dear Sabina, you can be certain I am too.

SABINA: And if you continue to love me, you can have everything you want.

FERDINANDO: I don't love you simply because of that. My love isn't mercenary; it's unselfish and disinterested. I love you because you deserve it . . . because you're so adorable.

SABINA: (*Weeping.*) My dearest, take my watch and keep it. I give it to you. Listen, I still have my dowry of ten thousand crowns. My husband and I had no children, and the ten thousand is all mine. If you continue to be fond of me, one day it will be all yours. I must tell you a little secret—I'm a bit older than you, you know.

FERDINANDO: You don't intend to marry again?

SABINA: Naughty boy, why do you think I'm so fond of you? Do you think I'm a wanton hussy? I wouldn't behave the way I do with you if I didn't intend to marry you.

FERDINANDO: My dear Sabina, that would be the happiest day of my life.

SABINA: My precious, wish it and it's quickly done.

FERDINANDO: So you have ten thousand crowns?

SABINA: Yes, and what's more, for the six years I've been a widow, I've accumulated all the interest too.

FERDINANDO: And it's all yours?

SABINA: All mine! To do with as I like!

FERDINANDO: So you could make a little settlement on me.

SABINA: Settlement? You're asking for a settlement? Am I so decrepit I can't get a husband without a settlement?

FERDINANDO: But didn't you say that one day your dowry will be all mine?

SABINA: Yes—after my death.

FERDINANDO: What's the difference—before or after?

SABINA: What if we have children?

FERDINANDO: You're still hoping to squeeze out a child?

SABINA: Tell me, little boy, is this the love you call unselfish?

FERDINANDO: It is unselfish. I could double my dear wife's money for her if I had a settlement to invest in a little shop in Livorno.

SABINA: (*Weeping.*) No, you miserable scrounger, you don't love me for myself.

FERDINANDO: If you don't believe I love you, I'll do something desperate.

SABINA: Oh no, dear, don't do that. I believe you. Bless your heart.

FERDINANDO: My love for you is so great it's tearing me to pieces. If you don't believe me, I'll kill myself.

SABINA: I believe it, I believe it! But don't ask me to give you a settlement. Isn't it enough to give you my heart?

FERDINANDO: There ought to be a little something on the side.

(Filippo enters.)

FILIPPO: Well, Ferdinando, shall we have a game of picchetto?

SABINA: Don't bother us.

FILIPPO: I'm not talking to you. I'm asking Ferdinando.

SABINA: Ferdinando doesn't want to play. Do you?

FERDINANDO: (*Rising.*) Pardon me.

FILIPPO: (*To Ferdinando.*) Do you want to play or not?

FERDINANDO: (*In a hurry to go.*) With your permission.

FILIPPO: Where are you going?

FERDINANDO: With your permission . . . ! (*He is gone.*)

SABINA: Let him go. He has to run. He took some rhubarb.

FILIPPO: He eats like a horse and overloads his stomach.

SABINA: That's not so. He's delicate. Every little mouthful disagrees with him.

FILIPPO: Where did he get the rhubarb?

SABINA: At the druggist's.

FILIPPO: No, he didn't. I was with the druggist till just now, playing cards, and Ferdinando wasn't there.

SABINA: You're going blind. You just didn't see him.

FILIPPO: I see better than you do.

SABINA: Ferdinando is incapable of telling lies.

FILIPPO: You know the only time he tells the truth? When he tells everybody that you're a loony old woman. (*He leaves.*)

SABINA: Liar! Snot-nose! Old devil! (*Giacinta enters. Sabina continues to shout at Filippo offstage:*) I know why you say that! I know why you persecute him! Because I love him and I'm going to marry him in spite of you and everybody else!

(*She pushes past Guglielmo, who is just entering.*)

GUGLIELMO: Why do you run away from me, Giacinta?

GIACINTA: I'm not running away. I'm going about my own business, doing what I have to do.

GUGLIELMO: And I'm rash enough to follow you . . . everywhere. A woman not so kind as you would have chased me away . . . long ago. I can't leave, I can't let go of you. I've tried—and I can't. But you are kind enough to put up with me. You understand the passion that's burning me up—consuming me—and you are charitable. If I thought you truly hated me or that my presence troubled you in any way, I would leave this instant, whatever the pain. But I have searched myself and I see nothing in my conduct so evil . . . that it could harm you . . . or hurt you.

GIACINTA: You have done more damage that you know.

GUGLIELMO: Have some pity on me. Talk to me. Just a word or two.

GIACINTA: This year we can't complain of the weather. It's perfect for the country.

GUGLIELMO: You are changing the subject.

GIACINTA: What did you think of supper last night at Leonardo's?

GUGLIELMO: I saw nothing but you.

GIACINTA: I hope our dinner today will be as pleasing as the hospitality we enjoyed last night.

GUGLIELMO: You are exquisite in everything you do. The pleasure of being with you is sharp and pure, like a knife. If I am depressed, that's my fault, no one else's, certainly not yours. Oh, forgive me! Will you allow me to say one thing?

GIACINTA: (*With some heat.*) It seems to me that so far you have said whatever you liked.

GUGLIELMO: Don't be angry with me. I couldn't bear that. I'll be silent if you tell me to.

GIACINTA: What is it you want to say?

GUGLIELMO: Now I am more miserable than ever! I see that my words irritate you. I'll go. I'll remove the irritation. I'll relieve you of my tormenting presence.

GIACINTA: What did you want to say to me?

GUGLIELMO: You permit me to speak?

GIACINTA: If you have something to say, say it!

GUGLIELMO: I know my place. Don't be afraid I'll say anything rash. I wouldn't take such advantage of your kindness. I'll only say that I love you . . . but if my love should cast the slightest shadow on your happiness or your peace of mind, I am prepared to sacrifice myself in any way you say . . . to please you.

GIACINTA: What can I say? How can I answer that?

GUGLIELMO: Have I said anything so bad that I don't deserve a response?

GIACINTA: Another man's promised bride should not respond to such talk.

GUGLIELMO: On the contrary—she can and she should. Freely and openly.

GIACINTA: I think I hear someone coming.

GUGLIELMO: Yes . . . guests arriving. Answer me. Give me just one word.

GIACINTA: It's Costanza and her niece.

GUGLIELMO: I shall go on begging till you answer me.

GIACINTA: Please! I'm so confused I don't know how to greet my guests.

(Enter Costanza, Rosina, and Tognino.)

(Guglielmo retires to one side.)

COSTANZA: Your servant, Giacinta.

GIACINTA: Your servant, Costanza.

ROSINA: Your devoted servant.

GIACINTA: Your servant, Rosina.

TOGNINO: Your servant.

GIACINTA: Tognino . . . you are welcome.

COSTANZA: We are disturbing you.

GIACINTA: Not at all. We are delighted to have you. I'm sorry you will not be better entertained.

COSTANZA: Oh, how can you say that? I have enjoyed your lavish hospitality on other occasions.

GIACINTA: Please sit down. (*To Guglielmo.*) Do join us. Here is a vacant seat by me.

GUGLIELMO: That is not for me.

GIACINTA: Why not?

GUGLIELMO: The man who has more right to it than I will soon be here.

GIACINTA: Please sit down. I beg you.

GUGLIELMO: (*Sitting.*) I do whatever you say. I obey you, always.

GIACINTA: How are you, Tognino?

TOGNINO: Fine.

GIACINTA: And how is your father?

TOGNINO: Fine.

GIACINTA: I hear he's gone to Maremma.

TOGNINO: M-hm.

(*Pause.*)

COSTANZA: I see you're wearing the new *mariage* fashion, Giacinta.

GIACINTA: Oh, it's just a plain little thing.

COSTANZA: Yes . . . it's nice though—for what it is. I'm glad you don't put on airs about it. Vittoria has one a hundred times worse than yours, and you'd think to hear her talk it was something wonderful.

(*A small pause.*)

GIACINTA: Would you like to play cards? Do you play ombre, Costanza?

COSTANZA: Of course.

GIACINTA: And Rosina?

ROSINA: All right.

GIACINTA: Tognino?

TOGNINO: I only play bazzica.

GIACINTA: Do you play bazzica, Rosina?

ROSINA: Why should I?

GIACINTA: I don't know. I'm simply trying to please you. I wouldn't want anybody to be unhappy. If you'd like to play with Tognino . . .

ROSINA: Why? We don't have to play together.

COSTANZA: Giacinta's being tactful, Rosina. We all understand one another. But Tognino doesn't have to play. He can watch Rosina and learn the game that way. Sit up straight, Tognino.

GIACINTA: You understand—don't you, Costanza?—how hard it is to get people at the right tables.

COSTANZA: Oh I know! I know from experience—trying to put together a table where people won't scratch each other's eyes out. Sometimes there's some grudge or jealousy I don't know about, and they frip and they frap and I haven't the slightest idea why. One has a headache and another has a bellyache, and you're worn out getting two little games going. Somebody says, "Tonight I want to be so-and-so's partner." Or another says, "Listen, I warn you, don't put me at a table with him or her; I don't want to go near them." Still, I don't mind so much when they come right out and say so. The worst is when they expect you to guess how they feel. It keeps you on your toes, remembering who is friend and who is foe. Trying to get the good players at one table and the duffers at another. Choosing the game that will suit each group best. Dividing them into those who leave early and those who stay on forever. Sometimes you have to keep the wife in one room and the husband in another.

GIACINTA: Yes, I have the same trouble. I believe I hear a carriage. It must be Vittoria and Leonardo. (*To Guglielmo.*) Would you do me a favor and go see if it is?

GUGLIELMO: (*Rising.*) I was right, you see. This seat is not for me.

GIACINTA: If you don't want to go . . .

GUGLIELMO: Don't worry. I'll be a good boy and do my duty. (*He goes out.*)

(*Pause.*)

GIACINTA: (*Trying to regain her composure.*) I expect we're going to have stormy weather.

COSTANZA: Tell me, Giacinta, has Guglielmo proposed to Vittoria?

GIACINTA: So people say.

COSTANZA: If she's going to be your sister-in-law, you should be the first to know.

GIACINTA: So far she hasn't taken me into her confidence.

COSTANZA: (*Knowingly.*) Oh . . . ! How about you and Leonardo—are you planning an early wedding?

GIACINTA: I really can't say. (*Launching into the offensive.*) And you, Costanza, when is your Rosina getting married?

COSTANZA: (*On the defensive.*) Who knows? It could happen.

ROSINA: Nobody would want to marry me.

TOGNINO: (*Whispering, and shoving Rosina.*) What do you mean— nobody?

ROSINA: (*Whispering to Tognino.*) Be quiet.

GIACINTA: (*Indicating Tognino.*) It seems to me, if I'm not mistaken . . .

COSTANZA: (*Laughing slyly.*) Do you really think so?

ROSINA: Sometimes appearances are deceiving.

GIACINTA: Tognino is not a young man who would joke about such things.

TOGNINO: Oh no?

(*He pokes Rosina and laughs, then rises and moves around the room in awkward embarrassment.*)

GIACINTA: He seems such a nice boy.

COSTANZA: (*Confidentially.*) He's not too bright.

GIACINTA: What does it matter, as long as he can support her?

COSTANZA: Oh yes, he can do that. He's an only son.

(*Enter Vittoria, on Guglielmo's arm, and Leonardo. Everyone rises and Giacinta goes to meet Vittoria.*)

GIACINTA: Your servant, Vittoria.

VITTORIA: Your servant, Giacinta.

(They kiss.)

LEONARDO: Please forgive me, Giacinta, if I'm late today. I had some business at home that delayed me. I trust you won't think I'm lacking in concern for you.

GIACINTA: I hope I've never given you cause to think me demanding. I'm delighted when you can come. When you cannot, I don't expect it of you.

LEONARDO: Not demanding, no. Just . . . concerned about me.

GIACINTA: Please sit down. (*Costanza, Rosina, and Tognino resume their places.*) Guglielmo, why don't you sit by Vittoria?

GUGLIELMO: Just as you say.

(He sits beside Vittoria. Giacinta sits by Guglielmo and Leonardo by Giacinta.)

VITTORIA: Guglielmo hasn't been by our house today.

GUGLIELMO: I couldn't get away.

VITTORIA: Yes, I know you've been here all day.

GUGLIELMO: I had some letters to write.

VITTORIA: We have ink and paper in our house too.

GUGLIELMO: I would never take such liberty.

VITTORIA: (*Disdainfully.*) Yes, dear, I understand.

GIACINTA: Vittoria, it's not necessary to be so punctilious.

LEONARDO: Learn from Giacinta. She's very easy going. She never complains if I don't call.

GIACINTA: I know some men don't want to bother.

LEONARDO: On the other hand, some are glad to be missed. They take it as a sign of affection.

GIACINTA: People differ. I prefer to be sincere.

LEONARDO: Now that I know your mind, I'll worry much less about calling on you regularly.

GIACINTA: You are your own master; you can do as you like.

(Sabina comes in on Ferdinando's arm.)

TOGNINO: (*Nudging Rosina.*) Hey, the old lady.

ROSINA: (*Quietly, to Costanza.*) The old lady.

COSTANZA: (*Whispering, to Rosina.*) Yes, with her darling.

SABINA: Your most humble servant, ladies and gentlemen.

VITTORIA: Your servant.

COSTANZA: My respects.

ROSINA: How are you?

SABINA: Very well. I'm very well. What delightful company! (*Nodding toward Tognino.*) Who is this young man?

TOGNINO: Your servant.

SABINA: My compliments, dear. Who are you?

ROSINA: Don't you recognize him? He's the doctor's son.

SABINA: What doctor?

COSTANZA: The doctor here in Montenero. Our doctor.

SABINA: Oh, good, good, I'm glad to hear it. What a fine, strapping young man! Is he married?

ROSINA: No, he's not.

SABINA: (*To Tognino.*) How old are you?

TOGNINO: Sixteen.

SABINA: Why don't you come to see us?

ROSINA: He's busy.

COSTANZA: He has to study.

ROSINA: He doesn't go anywhere.

SABINA: (*Leering.*) Yes, yes, I see—you keep him busy! Good for you both! I won't say a word, you needn't fear. I'm not one of your gossips. Ferdinando.

FERDINANDO: Yes?

SABINA: My precious, give me the handkerchief.

FERDINANDO: The white one?

SABINA: Yes, the white one. Last night I caught a little cold in this eye. It's running a bit.

FERDINANDO: Here you are.

(With some revulsion he hands her a handkerchief.)

SABINA: You seem upset. What's the matter?

FERDINANDO: Nothing, nothing at all.

SABINA: Are you jealous because I talked to that attractive young man?

LEONARDO: No, indeed. I simply hate being made a fool of in public.

SABINA: Don't be jealous, dear. I won't talk to anybody any more.

FERDINANDO: Talk to the devil, I don't care.

SABINA: Take the handkerchief.

FERDINANDO: (*Muttering as he takes it with distaste.*) I'll take ten thousand crowns as well.

SABINA: Not all of it! A little something, maybe. We'll see.

GIACINTA: Well now, ladies and gentlemen, shall we have a game?

VITTORIA: I'll do whatever the others do.

COSTANZA: You decide, Giacinta.

SABINA: You don't have to choose for me. I have my partner.

GIACINTA: What will you play, aunt?

SABINA: Tresette with Ferdinando.

FERDINANDO: Oh Lord, not tresette! It's so boring!

SABINA: It is not; it's a marvelous game. Besides, you have to play with me.

FERDINANDO: All right, I give up! Patience, Ferdinando.

SABINA: (*To Giacinta.*) You hear? I have a partner.

GIACINTA: Very well. Vittoria, Costanza, and Guglielmo will play three-handed ombre.

COSTANZA: (*In a mocking aside to Rosina.*) She didn't have to put me at the same table with the lady of the *mariage*.

VITTORIA: (*To Leonardo.*) Me play with her! Your bride-to-be doesn't know how to arrange a card-game.

GUGLIELMO: (*To Giacinta.*) I'm not worthy of sitting with you?

GIACINTA: (*To Guglielmo.*) I'm amazed at your temerity. (*To the others.*) We'll have another game of ombre—Leonardo, Rosina, and I.

ROSINA: Just as you say. (*To Costanza.*) This may turn into quite an entertaining scene for me!

GIACINTA: Is that all right with you, Leonardo?

LEONARDO: I don't care one way or the other.

GIACINTA: If you'd rather play at one of the other tables, say so.

LEONARDO: That's up to you.

GIACINTA: I can't read people's minds.

LEONARDO: I want only to please you. But that seems to be very difficult.

GIACINTA: It's much easier than you think.

VITTORIA: (*To Guglielmo.*) You seem a little glum.

GUGLIELMO: You know me. It's my nature.

VITTORIA: You are not a passionate lover then.

GUGLIELMO: More so than you think.

VITTORIA: Oh! How gallant of you!

GIACINTA: (*To Guglielmo.*) Good. I'm relieved to hear that you love Vittoria.

GUGLIELMO: (*To Giacinta quietly.*) That's one interpretation. There are others.

LEONARDO: (*To Giacinta.*) What did you say to Guglielmo?

GIACINTA: (*To Leonardo.*) Do I have to account for every word I speak?

LEONARDO: (*To Giacinta.*) Things seem a trifle too confidential.

GIACINTA: (*To Leonardo.*) You're not helping at all with these hurtful suspicions.

LEONARDO: Mine is a hurtful position—much too hurtful.

GIACINTA: Well, we're ready, ladies and gentlemen. If we don't hurry, dinner will be on the table.

SABINA: I'm ready. Come, Ferdinandino.

FERDINANDO: Here I am, always obedient. Just one game, eh?

(They sit at the card table in back.)

VITTORIA: If you please, Guglielmo.

GUGLIELMO: At your service.

VITTORIA: Do sit down, Costanza.

COSTANZA: Oh, you want to be in the middle to show off your beautiful dress?

(They sit at another card table.)

GIACINTA: If you're ready, Rosina.

ROSINA: Here I am. Tognino, come with me.

TOGNINO: I'd rather eat.

(They all sit and begin their games. Filippo enters.)

FILIPPO: Your servant, ladies and gentlemen. (*As all return the greeting without getting up.*) Playing already? Isn't there a place for me?

GIACINTA: Do you want to play, father?

FILIPPO: I should think so!

GIACINTA: There's another table. Go play bazzica with Tognino.

FILIPPO: Bazzica?

GIACINTA: That's the only game Tognino knows.

FILIPPO: Can't I play picchetto with Ferdinando?

SABINA: Ferdinando is taken.

FILIPPO: Oh. The honorable gentleman said he would play with me.

ROSINA: Signor Filippo, you're not ashamed to play with Tognino, are you?

FILIPPO: There's no choice. (*To Tognino.*) All right, let's play bazzica.

TOGNINO: I never play for more than a soldo a game.

FILIPPO: All right, all right. We'll play for a soldo. (*Going to the Servant, busy at the sideboard.*) Hey, listen, go to the kitchen and tell the cook to hurry up and put dinner on the table even if it's raw. (*The servant leaves.*) Play bazzica for an hour with this blockhead? Not me!

(Filippo sits down to play with Tognino.)

VITTORIA: (*To Guglielmo.*) You could have come by to say hello this morning.

GUGLIELMO: Didn't I say I never left the house?

VITTORIA: Yes. You did. You seem glad to stay here. I suspect you may be a little too attached to this house.

GUGLIELMO: I don't know what makes you say that.

COSTANZA: Are we playing or aren't we?

GUGLIELMO: Costanza is right.

VITTORIA: I may just throw down this hand.

GIACINTA: Vittoria seems to want to make a scene.

LEONARDO: Why don't you watch what you're playing, Giacinta?

ROSINA: Your turn, I played spades.

GIACINTA: My turn? There.

ROSINA: What! You just reneged.

LEONARDO: You don't want to renege! Your mind is not on the game.

GIACINTA: I'm doing my best. I hear you complaining but I don't know what about.

LEONARDO: I see no end to this damned stay in the country.

SABINA: (*Gloating.*) Ha ha! I beat him! I beat him! I beat him!

FERDINANDO: Nice work. You beat me.

VITTORIA: (*To Guglielmo.*) Giacinta is watching us like a hawk.

GUGLIELMO: The hostess has to keep an eye on everything.

VITTORIA: That's right, stand up for her. (*Slapping down a card viciously.*) Trumps.

COSTANZA: That's not a trump.

VITTORIA: How the devil should I know?

COSTANZA: (*Loudly.*) Really! This is no way to play cards!

GIACINTA: What's the matter, Costanza?

COSTANZA: The things she does!

VITTORIA: (*Laughing.*) Stick to your own game, Giacinta.

GIACINTA: Sorry . . . when I hear someone complaining . . .

TOGNINO: Bazzicotto! Three of a kind!

FILIPPO: (*Furious.*) All right, all right! Bazzicotto, bazzicotto!

GIACINTA: (*Quietly to Leonardo.*) It seems Vittoria is not feeling very friendly toward me.

LEONARDO: (*To Giacinta.*) What can I say? She'll be marrying soon.

GIACINTA: When?

LEONARDO: It could be very shortly.

GIACINTA: You're counting on Guglielmo to marry her?

LEONARDO: If he doesn't, he won't be at your house any more.

GIACINTA: Really?

LEONARDO: Really.

ROSINA: (*To Giacinta.*) Your turn.

VITTORIA: I think they're talking about me.

(*The Servant comes in.*)

SERVANT: Dinner is served.

(*The Servant leaves.*)

COSTANZA: (*Rising.*) Thank heaven.

SABINA: I want to finish this hand.

FILIPPO: (*Rising.*) Finish it by yourself then because we're eating.

FERDINANDO: (*Rising.*) With your permission. I have an appetite.

SABINA: (*Rising.*) Oh good, good. The rhubarb did its work.

TOGNINO: Three soldi, Signor Filippo.

FILIPPO: Here, take your three soldi. Let's go in.

GIACINTA: Dinner is on the table. Shall we go?

VITTORIA: Go ahead.

ROSINA: I'm certainly not going in first.

SABINA: Well then, I'll go. Your arm, Ferdinando.

FERDINANDO: (*Offering his arm.*) At your service.

SABINA: (*Curtsying.*) By your leave.

FERDINANDO: (*Leaving with Sabina.*) It's my lucky day.

GIACINTA: After you, Vittoria.

VITTORIA: (*To Guglielmo.*) May I have your arm?

GUGLIELMO: (*Offering his arm.*) At your service.

VITTORIA: Sorry you have to suffer with me.

GUGLIELMO: I suffer? (*Looking back to Giacinta.*) Far more than she thinks.

(*He goes out with Vittoria.*)

GIACINTA: (*To Costanza and Rosina.*) After you, ladies.

COSTANZA: Go ahead, Rosina.

ROSINA: Come, Tognino.

TOGNINO: I could eat a cow.

(*He leaves with Rosina.*)

COSTANZA: (*To Giacinta.*) By your leave.

FILIPPO: (*To Costanza.*) May I have the honor?

COSTANZA: How kind of you.

FILIPPO: If you don't mind.

COSTANZA: It's a pleasure.

FILIPPO: A treat for this poor old man.

COSTANZA: (*As she takes his arm.*) Poor Filippo! Something even for him.

(*They leave.*)

GIACINTA: (*To Leonardo.*) Shall we go in?

LEONARDO: May I offer you my arm?

GIACINTA: Not if I don't deserve it.

LEONARDO: You're very hard on me.

GIACINTA: Please, Leonardo. Let's not bicker.

LEONARDO: I love you entirely too much, Giacinta.

GIACINTA: Yes, more than I deserve.

LEONARDO: And you love me very little.

GIACINTA: I love you as much as I know how . . . as much as I can.

LEONARDO: Don't leave me hopeless.

GIACINTA: Let's not have a scene, shall we?

(She takes him forcefully by the arm to lead him out.)

LEONARDO: (*To himself.*) Cruel fate!

GIACINTA: (*To herself.*) Oh, love . . . duty . . . damned vacation in the country!

Scene 2

A wood.
Brigida and Paolino enter.

BRIGIDA: Here . . . here, Paolino. Let's stop here and cool off a bit.

PAOLINO: The master may be looking for me, and if he doesn't find me . . .

BRIGIDA: They're all playing cards. Then they'll have their coffee and play some more. Stay awhile . . . unless you don't like my company.

PAOLINO: Brigida, you know I like you very much.

BRIGIDA: Actually I'd like to stay out here with you awhile.

PAOLINO: You have to admit in the country it's easier to get a few minutes, even a few hours off. And there are more places to be alone with somebody.

BRIGIDA: They manage it, don't they?—our masters and mistresses. We can do the same.

PAOLINO: Yes, that's true. Things happen in the country that couldn't happen so easily in town.

BRIGIDA: (*Chuckling.*) Something occurred here to my mistress she won't soon forget.

PAOLINO: What was that?

BRIGIDA: Sorry, I can't tell you. It would curl your hair.

PAOLINO: Something certainly must have happened to agitate my master and your mistress. I stood behind them, serving at the dining table, you know. They didn't eat an ounce of food between them.

BRIGIDA: Who sat on the other side of my mistress?

PAOLINO: Signor Guglielmo.

BRIGIDA: Damn him, he'll be the ruin of everybody in the house.

PAOLINO: Is something going on between him and your mistress?

BRIGIDA: No, not a thing. Where was Vittoria?

PAOLINO: Next to Signor Guglielmo.

BRIGIDA: The nerve of that snake in the grass!

PAOLINO: Why?

BRIGIDA: Putting himself between those two.

PAOLINO: Every now and then he'd whisper something to your mistress in that long-suffering way of his, but I couldn't hear what he said.

BRIGIDA: Did Signor Leonardo notice?

PAOLINO: Once I think he did, because he handed me his plate so abruptly that he hit her shoulder and spotted her dress.

BRIGIDA: Spotted her new dress? She must have been furious.

PAOLINO: No, she hardly seemed to notice.

BRIGIDA: That's a wonder. She must have had a lot of other things on her mind.

PAOLINO: My master tried to clean it off and she wouldn't let him.

BRIGIDA: Her dress . . . and keeping it fresh—that's her grand passion. Poor girl! She really must be upset.

PAOLINO: I'll bet she's fallen for Signor Guglielmo.

BRIGIDA: Get out! What the devil do you mean? What makes you think that? Isn't she engaged to Signor Leonardo? Isn't Signor Guglielmo courting your mistress Vittoria?

PAOLINO: Oh, I think my mistress is fooling herself. All through dinner she pestered Signor Guglielmo and he never once answered her. He never paid any attention to her at all.

BRIGIDA: Because he was talking to my mistress?

PAOLINO: Yes, whispering, and nudging her with his elbow—and sometimes with his foot.

BRIGIDA: The devil! If I'd been standing where you were, I don't know if I could have resisted bouncing a plate off his skull.

PAOLINO: What did I tell you? If there wasn't something between them you wouldn't be so excited.

BRIGIDA: Let's talk about something else. I suppose the old lady sat next to that sly fox Ferdinando.

PAOLINO: Of course, and she shouted tender little nothings in his hairy ear while he wolfed down all the food within reach. You'd have thought he hadn't eaten for four days.

BRIGIDA: And my poor mistress ate nothing?

PAOLINO: How could she eat, trapped there between her fiancé and her lover?

BRIGIDA: Enough of that. How did Costanza and her niece Rosina behave?

PAOLINO: They did well for themselves, but the one who really tucked away the food, almost as much as Ferdinando, was that fool Tognino.

BRIGIDA: Was he seated next to his Rosina?

PAOLINO: Naturally, and how they enjoyed it! The way they whispered was enough to turn your stomach.

BRIGIDA: There's another marriage in the offing.

PAOLINO: So it seems.

BRIGIDA: Their romance happened in the country too. If Rosina hadn't come here, she would have had a hard time finding a husband in Livorno. But you know, in all the years I've been coming here, I'm still single. Either that's what I deserve or I'm just unlucky.

PAOLINO: Brigida . . . do you want to be married?

BRIGIDA: As much as any other girl. I'm not a nun.

PAOLINO: Seek and ye shall find.

BRIGIDA: I don't know about that—I haven't found. But I'm still young—maybe not beautiful, but I'm not exactly deformed. I have as much ability as any other girl, and maybe more than some. As for dowry, in money and things I'm worth three or four hundred crowns. Yet no one is panting for me. No one . . . wants me.

PAOLINO: I'm sorry. I have to go, or I'd have a word to say on the subject.

BRIGIDA: Say a word. Say two. Don't leave me curious.

PAOLINO: It's a shame for you to waste your time like this.

BRIGIDA: Do you have something particular in mind?

PAOLINO: Yes, I do . . . but . . .

BRIGIDA: But what?

PAOLINO: I don't know if you'd be interested.

BRIGIDA: If I can't have a good honest man like you, I'd rather stay as I am.

PAOLINO: Brigida . . . we'll talk about it.

BRIGIDA: This evening, while they're playing cards.

PAOLINO: Yes, we'll have all the time we want then. I'll drop over and we can come back here to the woods.

BRIGIDA: Oh . . . at night here in the woods . . . I don't know . . .

PAOLINO: I was joking. I'm a decent man and I respect you and I hope things will go well between us.

BRIGIDA: You make me so happy when you say that . . .

PAOLINO: Good-bye . . . good-bye . . . until tonight.

(He leaves, bowing to Giacinta, who is just entering.)

GIACINTA: I came to get a breath of air . . . and have a moment of quiet. How can anyone live here in the country? Will this vacation ever be over? A fine time we're having this year!

BRIGIDA: I don't know . . . The country this year may bring something good for me. *(She leaves.)*

(Giacinta paces back and forth, then sits.)

(Guglielmo enters.)

GUGLIELMO: I've finally found you.

GIACINTA: What do you want? Why do you follow me everywhere? Why don't you leave me alone?

GUGLIELMO: I will. I'll leave you, don't be afraid. Just allow me a few words.

GIACINTA: *(Looking around.)* Then hurry.

GUGLIELMO: Please . . . I beg you . . . answer me. Give me an answer to what I said to you this morning.

GIACINTA: I don't remember what it was.

GUGLIELMO: I'll repeat it.

GIACINTA: No! No, there's no need.

GUGLIELMO: Then you do remember.

GIACINTA: Please! Please go away and let me be.

GUGLIELMO: Two words and I'll go.

GIACINTA: Well?

GUGLIELMO: Must I live . . . or must I die?

GIACINTA: Why do you ask me that?

GUGLIELMO: You're the only one who can tell me. Tell me what I must do.

GIACINTA: Do you want me to break my promise to Leonardo? Are you asking me to disgrace myself before everyone?

GUGLIELMO: I can ask nothing. I can only beg.

GIACINTA: You could be silent.

GUGLIELMO: No. No, I can't do that. Not until I know.

GIACINTA: Well then, if we must, let's talk about it. You and I, Guglielmo, are both unhappy—and for the same reason. Unhappiness we could bear, but the worst of it is we're about to lose everything—our self-respect, our reputations, even our honor. I fail in my duty when I listen to you; you fail in yours when you follow me and insinuate yourself into my feelings. I let my father down, I let my future husband down, and I let myself down. Then how can I call myself a decent girl? And you betray your friends and your host—my father! You betray Leonardo. You deceive his sister Vittoria. And for what? What can we expect from such shameful behavior? Think what you're doing! And think about me. If it's true that you love me, don't try to ruin me, for the love of God! Can love be that cruel? Do you want to hurt a girl who is weak enough to love you? Yes, I confess that I love you. I admit it to my shame—and in spite of myself. I love you. But this confession is all you will get from me. I intend to do everything I can to forget you, or else I'll let this infatuation destroy me and I'll die. We must part for good. If you persist, I'll find ways to hurt you and humiliate you. I intend to do my duty whether or not you do yours. You wanted to know how I felt and I've told you. You ask if you must live or die. I don't know. I can't even say what will become of me. But honor comes first.

GUGLIELMO: I don't know how to answer that.

GIACINTA: I didn't know how to say it. It wasn't easy.

(A long silence.)

(Enter Leonardo.)

LEONARDO: Here you are. What's the secret between you two? (*To Giacinta.*) Why do you come here with Guglielmo?

GIACINTA: There's no secret. It's something that concerns you more than it does me. When you asked me to be your wife, you made the concerns of your family my own. People are saying that there is an attachment between Guglielmo and your sister Vittoria. I know that she favors him; she has shown it, publicly. These are very delicate matters that affect a girl's good name. I didn't know precisely what Guglielmo's intentions were, but he has just reassured me. He realizes that a man of honor must not take advantage of a decent girl. He recognizes his duty; he respects her as she deserves—as the dignity of your family deserves; and if you will give your consent, through me he asks you for Vittoria as his wife.

LEONARDO: He asks through you?

GIACINTA: Yes, through me.

LEONARDO: Why? Was there no other intermediary in the world besides you?

GIACINTA: I am the one who confronted him. As your future wife, it was only right that I should take on the task. Guglielmo knows what I said to him, and on a man of honor, an honest man, a gentle man like Guglielmo my words must have had some effect.

LEONARDO: What does Guglielmo have to say?

GUGLIELMO: If you consider me worthy, I ask for your sister as my wife.

LEONARDO: I'll give you an answer this evening.

GIACINTA: Why can't you give him an answer now?

LEONARDO: I must talk to my sister first.

GIACINTA: She's bound to be happy about such a proposal from a man like Guglielmo!

LEONARDO: (*To Giacinta.*) Let's go. They're waiting for us to join them in a walk.

GIACINTA: All right, I'm ready. Let's go.

LEONARDO: Do you want to take my arm?

GIACINTA: I'm surprised that you ask me that. Do we need these formalities, you and I? If you don't offer me your arm, who will?

LEONARDO: You came here without me.

GIACINTA: And now I want to go back with you.

(With determination she takes his arm.)

LEONARDO: I'm still not sure why.

(They leave.)

(Guglielmo hangs back for a moment before he slowly follows them off.)

Scene 3

The study in Filippo's villa.
Filippo and Vittoria.

VITTORIA: If you don't mind, I'd like to ask you something, here where no one can hear us.

FILIPPO: Gladly. I was just standing around in the game room twiddling my thumbs. They're playing faro, and that's not my game.

VITTORIA: Can you tell me where Giacinta is at the moment?

FILIPPO: I really don't know. I haven't been checking on her.

VITTORIA: And where is Guglielmo?

FILIPPO: I know even less about him. Do you expect me to keep track of everybody in the house?

VITTORIA: The point is—they're both missing.

FILIPPO: Both who?

VITTORIA: Guglielmo and Giacinta.

FILIPPO: So? Probably one here, one there.

VITTORIA: They may be together.

FILIPPO: Oh, I see. Well, my daughter is no hussy.

VITTORIA: I didn't say she was. But I can tell you that at the gaming tables in there, that's all they're talking about. And since they have both disappeared . . .

FILIPPO: Disappeared?

VITTORIA: They're nowhere in sight; nobody knows where they are.

FILIPPO: Well—what does your brother Leonardo say?

VITTORIA: He's gone to look for them.

FILIPPO: If I find out . . . ! If they're . . . ! I'm going this very minute. But here's Leonardo. Perhaps he found them.

(Leonardo enters.)

LEONARDO: Signor Filippo, may I write a letter?

FILIPPO: Sit right here. There's paper in the drawer, and here's pen and ink.

VITTORIA: Leonardo, you look upset. Has something happened?

FILIPPO: Do you know where my daughter is?

LEONARDO: *(Sitting at the desk.)* Yes, I do.

FILIPPO: Where is she?

LEONARDO: In the game room.

FILIPPO: Where has she been?

LEONARDO: She went to see the foreman's wife, who is sick with the fever.

FILIPPO: Who went with her?

LEONARDO: No one.

FILIPPO: She went alone?

LEONARDO: (*Writing.*) Yes.

FILIPPO: Guglielmo didn't go with her?

LEONARDO: Why should he? Can't she go see the foreman's wife by herself? If she needed someone, she could call on me.

FILIPPO: You see, Vittoria?

VITTORIA: (*To Leonardo.*) You heard what they were saying in the game room. I could see you were furious.

LEONARDO: People jump to conclusions. I went to look for her myself, and I found her with the foreman's wife and brought her back to the villa.

(*He continues writing his letter.*)

FILIPPO: You hear, Vittoria? My daughter is not the kind . . .

VITTORIA: (*To Leonardo.*) Has Guglielmo come back?

LEONARDO: (*Writing.*) He's back.

VITTORIA: Where had he been?

LEONARDO: I don't know.

VITTORIA: (*Sarcastically.*) Probably visiting the foreman.

LEONARDO: (*Still writing.*) Charity, sister, charity.

VITTORIA: I was never over-trusting, and I wouldn't advise you to be.

LEONARDO: Let me finish this letter.

VITTORIA: Are you writing Livorno?

LEONARDO: I'm writing where I want to write. Signor Filippo, may I ask a favor? Could you send someone to find my manservant and tell him to come to me at once? If he doesn't find me here, I'll be at the coffee shop. Tell him not to fail.

FILIPPO: I'll do it right away. Vittoria, a word to the wise: don't you be so eager to jump to the worst conclusions about me and my family. (*He leaves.*)

LEONARDO: Good advice.

VITTORIA: Tell me, brother, do you like the way Giacinta is behaving? Are you happy with the way things look?

LEONARDO: (*Writing.*) I'm completely happy.

VITTORIA: You couldn't be! Even with Guglielmo?

LEONARDO: (*Writing.*) Even with him.

VITTORIA: You think he's behaving well?

LEONARDO: (*Writing.*) Guglielmo is a gentleman and a man of honor.

VITTORIA: Well, I know from all I've heard and seen . . .

LEONARDO: (*Irritated.*) Let me write this letter. You're bothering me.

VITTORIA: Listen to me! Just one moment! Then I'll leave you alone!

LEONARDO: (*Writing.*) What is it?

VITTORIA: Did Guglielmo tell you he liked me?

LEONARDO: (*Writing.*) Yes.

VITTORIA: Do you believe him?

LEONARDO: (*Writing.*) I believe him.

VITTORIA: You do?!

LEONARDO: (*Writing.*) Oh shut up.

VITTORIA: Has he brought it up again?

LEONARDO: Yes, he has.

VITTORIA: He has?

LEONARDO: Yes. Now let me finish.

VITTORIA: And you never said a word to me?

LEONARDO: I'll tell you all about it if you'll let me finish this letter.

VITTORIA: Finish it, finish it! I don't know what to believe. Maybe I was mistaken. Maybe it was just jealousy. When did Guglielmo say that?

LEONARDO: If you could just be quiet for one minute . . . (*Looking over the letter.*) An important letter takes concentration, and you're pestering me.

VITTORIA: I'm dying to know.

LEONARDO: (*Referring to the letter.*) Yes . . . yes, that should sound natural enough.

(*Brigida enters.*)

BRIGIDA: They have finished the card games and are getting ready to go out for coffee. They sent me to ask if you'd like to come along.

LEONARDO: (*Rising.*) We're coming.

VITTORIA: Aren't you going to tell me?

LEONARDO: I'll tell you this evening.

VITTORIA: Give me at least an inkling of what he said.

LEONARDO: This is not the time or place.

VITTORIA: I can't wait.

LEONARDO: Vittoria, you miss so many chances to keep your mouth shut. (*He leaves.*)

VITTORIA: Brigida, tell me—where did your mistress go after dinner?

BRIGIDA: How should I know?

VITTORIA: How is the foreman's wife?

BRIGIDA: The foreman's wife? She's fine as far as I know.

VITTORIA: Doesn't she have the fever?

BRIGIDA: Fever? No, she was in the kitchen helping with dinner.

VITTORIA: I knew it! They're all lying to me. They're laughing at me, especially that brother of mine.

BRIGIDA: Aren't you going out for coffee?

VITTORIA: Did Guglielmo and Giacinta come back to the villa together?

BRIGIDA: I don't know. I don't know a thing about anything. I'm not the one to ask. My mistress is an honest and well-behaved young lady, and if there are young men up to no good, it's not the fault of well-brought-up young ladies. If you want to go for coffee, go; and if you don't, I've done my duty. (*She leaves.*)

(*Vittoria ponders for a moment and then strides purposefully out.*)

Scene 4

Countryside with a coffee shop and a few houses. Two or three benches for customers.
Tita and Beltrame, waiters.

BELTRAME: Tita, how's your appetite?

TITA: Oh, fine. I can't wait for supper.

BELTRAME: Today at Signor Filippo's we thought we would have a feast but there wasn't enough left over to feed a flea.

TITA: The plates came from the table clean as a whistle. There was hardly a bone.

BELTRAME: And of what little the guests left on their plates, how much ever reached us?

TITA: Not a thing. They all beat us to it. The foreman and his wife, the gardener, the washwoman—all the servants wanted theirs first.

BELTRAME: Of course they made a great show of making some soup for us out of the leftovers.

TITA: What soup! I think they made it out of the dishwater.

BELTRAME: The wine was even worse.

TITA: What you'd give to an invalid.

BELTRAME: At least there was some bread.

TITA: But you had to beg for it.

BELTRAME: I latched on to a nice piece of beef that was tender as butter, I have to tell you.

TITA: And I spied a capon thigh and a whole wing—untouched—and whacked them off in a jiffy.

BELTRAME: The macaroni wasn't bad.

TITA: I liked the meat balls too.

BELTRAME: If the roast had been hot it would have been hard to beat.

TITA: Well, it was milk-fed veal. I wrapped up a piece to eat later tonight.

BELTRAME: I took some cream cakes and a piece of parmigiano.

TITA: Oh, if it had been a real meal, as I said, we could have brought away a napkinful of food.

BELTRAME: If nobody had been looking.

TITA: As it was, if there was anything left on a plate, the house servants were right there to take it for fear we might slip some in our pockets.

BELTRAME: I never put food in my pocket—not the greasy kind.

TITA: Neither do I. I eat it on the spot.

BELTRAME: You pick up a little here, a little there. It keeps you alive.

TITA: Uh-oh. Here comes company. Let's go in.

BELTRAME: The old lady's out in front.

TITA: And how that old biddy can eat!

BELTRAME: How about Signor Ferdinando?

TITA: And your dear Signor Tognino?

BELTRAME: Hey, have you noticed how he behaves around that girl?

TITA: Have I!

BELTRAME: It looks like there'll be a big wedding—soon.

TITA: Of appetite and hunger.

BELTRAME: Or need and absolute necessity. They'd better hurry.

(The two waiters go into the coffee shop.)

(The following pairs come in: Sabina and Ferdinando, Giacinta and Leonardo, Vittoria and Guglielmo, Rosina and Tognino, Costanza and Filippo. They sit. A waiter [Tita or Beltrame] appears and takes their orders, going from one to the other.)

GIACINTA: Coffee.

LEONARDO: A glass of water.

ROSINA: Sherbet.

TOGNINO: Chocolate.

VITTORIA: Coffee—without sugar.

COSTANZA: Lemonade.

FILIPPO: Cider.

FERDINANDO: A glass of rosolio.

SABINA: Bring me some iced milk.

VITTORIA: (*To Guglielmo.*) Do you know what it is my brother has to tell me? Or don't you want to say either?

GUGLIELMO: Forgive me, but that's up to him. It's not my place to reveal it.

VITTORIA: If you were genuinely fond of me, you would be a little more obliging.

LEONARDO: (*To Giacinta.*) What's the matter?

GIACINTA: We shouldn't have come to this place. They make you wait half an hour for coffee.

LEONARDO: Be patient. There are ten of us and we all gave different orders.

GIACINTA: Patient. Yes, I know something about being patient.

ROSINA: (*To Tognino.*) Did you hear her? The princess wants immediate service.

TOGNINO: (*To Rosina.*) Oh, I forgot to order a couple of cakes.

ROSINA: Are you still hungry?

TOGNINO: Sure. I'm always hungry.

FILIPPO: You have nothing to say, Costanza?

COSTANZA: What do you want me to say?

FILIPPO: Tell me something—is it true your niece is in love with that simpleton Tognino?

COSTANZA: I don't know. To tell you the truth, I don't pay much attention. After all, she's my niece, not my daughter.

SABINA: (*To Ferdinando.*) It's getting damp. I wouldn't want to catch cold.

FERDINANDO: You poor thing! Cover up your head. Don't you have a hood?

SABINA: No. Wait. (*She takes out a little umbrella.*) Open this umbrella and hold it over me.

FERDINANDO: Do I have to stand here for half an hour like this?

SABINA: When you're fond of someone, nothing is tiresome or too much.

FERDINANDO: Then you must not be fond of me.

SABINA: Why?

FERDINANDO: Because giving me a miserable little settlement is too much for you.

SABINA: Are you still going on about that?

FERDINANDO: It's either a settlement or good-bye.

SABINA: (*Weeping.*) Oh you ungrateful wretch!

(*She wipes her eyes.*)

(*Tita and Beltrame bring the orders, make mistakes, get completely confused.*)

TOGNINO: The chocolate is for me.

ROSINA: Mine is the sherbet.

COSTANZA: Hey! Lemonade.

SABINA: That's my iced milk.

LEONARDO: A glass of water is what I ordered.

VITTORIA: No, no! Coffee!

GIACINTA: Coffee here, if you please. (*They give Giacinta the coffee.*) Dunces! I didn't order coffee without sugar!

FERDINANDO: Could I have that rosolio?

FILIPPO: Hey, waiter! Did someone tell you I was to be the last one served? If everybody has his order now, would you please bring me the cider I ordered?

(Paolino enters and discreetly catches Leonardo's attention.)

LEONARDO: (*To Giacinta as he rises.*) Excuse me. I must speak to my servant.

GIACINTA: Go ahead.

FERDINANDO: (*Rising.*) By your leave.

SABINA: Where are you going?

FERDINANDO: (*Taking Leonardo's seat.*) I'll be right back.

SABINA: The rogue! He loves me and yet he spites me all the time.

FERDINANDO: (*To Giacinta.*) I've had all I can take.

GIACINTA: (*To Ferdinando.*) I'm surprised at you, daring to ridicule my aunt. She may be old and silly but she's a decent woman.

FERDINANDO: I'm not ridiculing . . .

GIACINTA: (*Interrupting.*) Be quiet if you know what's good for you.

FERDINANDO: So, Rosina, are you having fun?

ROSINA: Leave me alone. I want nothing to do with you.

FERDINANDO: (*Resuming his seat by Sabina.*) Here I am again by your side, my precious.

SABINA: You don't deserve even a glance from me. But I haven't the heart to punish you.

LEONARDO: (*To Paolino.*) Have someone copy this letter, or do it yourself and disguise your handwriting. Seal it and address it to me. Then when we're back at the villa and about to start playing cards again, bring me the letter as if someone had just delivered it from Livorno. Quickly now. This is urgent.

PAOLINO: Very good. (*He leaves.*)

(*Giacinta rises and paces nervously. Guglielmo watches her.*)

LEONARDO: (*To Giacinta.*) You seem nervous.

GIACINTA: I can't breathe. It's so sultry.

LEONARDO: We'll go back to the villa, if you like.

VITTORIA: Yes, let's go, let's go.

(*She rises and they all follow.*)

SABINA: Let me go first. You know I've always been short-sighted. (*To Ferdinando.*) I don't want anyone to overhear us.

FERDINANDO: Yes, let's decide on the settlement.

SABINA: (*Taking his arm pettishly.*) You and your settlement!

(*They go out.*)

GIACINTA: Go ahead if you like.

VITTORIA: No, no, we'll go as we came.

LEONARDO: (*Giving Giacinta his arm.*) Let's not stand on ceremony.

GIACINTA: Heavens, it's hot.

(*She goes out with Leonardo.*)

VITTORIA: You look like bad news, Guglielmo.

GUGLIELMO: How so?

VITTORIA: You're so gloomy.

GUGLIELMO: That's my nature.

(He goes out with Vittoria.)

COSTANZA: Hey, Rosina, what are you looking at?

ROSINA: I see some huge clouds in the sky. Come, Tognino dear, let's hurry back.

(She leaves with Tognino.)

COSTANZA: Are you coming, Filippo?

FILIPPO: Yes, yes, here I am. Always the last one.

(He leaves with Costanza.)

Scene 5

> *The gaming room in Filippo's villa.*
> *Brigida and the Servant are lighting lamps and preparing the gaming tables.*

BRIGIDA: Quickly, light the lamps. They're coming; I see them through the window. I hope Paolino will come too. In the week that's left of vacation maybe he and I will come to an understanding. Oh, it would be wonderful if I got married before any of them! Listen, if Paolino comes, let me know. I'll take the ladies' mantles. Here they are.

(They all enter in the same order in which they left the last scene. Brigida takes the mantles, the Servant the hats.)

SABINA: Oof! I'm a little tired. (*To Ferdinando.*) Come here, you.

FERDINANDO: Here I am, here I am.

(He sits beside her.)

GIACINTA: Sit down, everybody.

(They all sit down, but there is no chair for Filippo.)

FILIPPO: No place for me?

BRIGIDA: I'll get you a chair, Signor Filippo. *(She brings him a chair.)*

FILIPPO: Yes, some charity for an old man.

BRIGIDA: There you are.

FILIPPO: Some day I may be master in my own house.

(He sits.)

VITTORIA: *(Rising.)* Brother, a word if you please.

LEONARDO: *(Rising.)* Yes?

VITTORIA: What were you going to tell me?

LEONARDO: I can say it in two words. Guglielmo has asked me for your hand in marriage.

VITTORIA: *(Turning to smile at Guglielmo.)* Really?

(Guglielmo looks away.)

LEONARDO: So now it's up to you.

VITTORIA: That makes me very happy.

LEONARDO: *(Calling.)* Guglielmo! Might we see you for a moment?

GUGLIELMO: Here I am.

(*Giacinta is straining to overhear them.*)

LEONARDO: My sister is pleased to hear of your good intentions and is ready to consent.

GUGLIELMO: Very well.

VITTORIA: Very well? Is that all you can say?

GUGLIELMO: What would you like me to say?

VITTORIA: What kind of man are you? I can never tell if you're happy or unhappy.

GUGLIELMO: You'll have to take me as I am.

VITTORIA: Perhaps you'll wake up once we are married.

LEONARDO: Signor Filippo, Signor Ferdinando, may I have a word with you?

FILIPPO: (*Rising and going to them.*) Gladly.

FERDINANDO: (*Coming forward.*) I'm at your service.

LEONARDO: Be good enough to act as witnesses to the mutual promise of marriage between Signor Guglielmo and my sister Vittoria.

(*Giacinta sits suddenly.*)

FILIPPO: Good! I'm glad to hear it.

FERDINANDO: Congratulations.

SABINA: (*To Ferdinando.*) You see how it's done.

FERDINANDO: Give me a settlement and we'll do it too.

SABINA: (*Sitting down.*) Damn your settlement!

LEONARDO: We'll draw up the marriage contract at once, and you gentlemen can witness it in writing.

FILIPPO: Yes, of course.

FERDINANDO: If you like, I can draw it up myself. I've done it before, for others. Then there will be no wait.

VITTORIA: You'll be doing us a favor.

LEONARDO: Yes, do that.

FERDINANDO: Right away. I'll be a guest at your wedding feast! (*He goes out.*)

VITTORIA: (*To Guglielmo.*) Have you nothing to say?

GUGLIELMO: I approve everything. What else is there to say?

VITTORIA: It seems you're acting more out of constraint than love.

GUGLIELMO: On the contrary, I'm doing what love constrains me to do.

VITTORIA: Now, that was nicely said! It's the second time you've confessed you love me. Let's sit down.

(*They all sit again.*)

COSTANZA: I'm very happy for you, Vittoria.

VITTORIA: Thank you.

ROSINA: Congratulations.

VITTORIA: Much obliged.

ROSINA: (*To Tognino.*) You see? They did it.

TOGNINO: (*Grinning.*) We'll do it too.

(Paolino enters, approaches Leonardo, and bows.)

LEONARDO: What is it?

PAOLINO: A special messenger from Livorno just brought this urgent letter for you.

LEONARDO: Let's see what it is. Give it to me. (*He rises and opens the letter. To Filippo:*) It's from Signor Fulgenzio.

FILIPPO: Our old friend? What does he say?

LEONARDO: Diamine! It's upsetting news. Listen to what he writes: "Dearest friend, I send you this message in haste expressly to advise you that your Uncle Bernardino has been brought down with a malady of the chest and in the past three days reduced to such extremes that the doctors give him only a few hours to live. He has sent for the notary, from which you can draw your own conclusions. Your inheritance is at stake, and I advise you to come at once to Livorno."

FILIPPO: Well, well! I would advise the same thing. Don't delay for a moment. They say he'll leave you over fifty thousand crowns.

VITTORIA: Yes, at once, at once, at once! I'll come with you!

LEONARDO: I'm sorry to have to leave such good company.

VITTORIA: I'm sure Guglielmo will come with us.

LEONARDO: Paolino, go and hire four horses at the post and have them get the carriage ready. There will be four of us—Signor Guglielmo, my sister, myself and you. Don't bother with the trunks.

PAOLINO: Very well.

BRIGIDA: Paolino . . .

PAOLINO: My girl . . . ?

BRIGIDA: You're going?

PAOLINO: Yes, but I'll be back for the trunks.

BRIGIDA: For the love of heaven, don't forget about me!

PAOLINO: No danger. I give you my word. (*He leaves.*)

(*Brigida follows him out.*)

FILIPPO: (*To Leonardo.*) When you get to Livorno, write us at once. Come back if you can. We'll wait for you here. If you can't come, we'll be returning soon ourselves.

VITTORIA: Let's not waste time! Giacinta, forgive our haste. Keep me in your good thoughts, and good-bye till we meet again in Livorno.

GIACINTA: Yes, my dearest, good-bye for now.

(*They kiss.*)

LEONARDO: (*To Vittoria.*) Don't you want to wait and sign the contract?

VITTORIA: Oh yes! That has to be signed. Hey! Ferdinando! Have you finished writing my marriage contract?

(*Ferdinando comes in.*)

FERDINANDO: Here I am, here I am. What's all this? You're going? You're leaving us?

VITTORIA: Have you finished writing the marriage contract for us?

FERDINANDO: Here it is, all done.

GUGLIELMO: Excuse me, but couldn't we do that later? Wouldn't it be better to have a notary draw it up in Livorno?

FERDINANDO: But it's already done!

GUGLIELMO: It has to be read, and signed, and witnessed. That will take time. Leonardo, I advise you to hurry. It would be much better to go now and leave the contract until we're back in town. After all, I'll be right there with you. We're all going back to Livorno together.

LEONARDO: True. Not a bad idea. Let's go. We'll do it in Livorno. (*Guglielmo can scarcely conceal his sigh of relief.*) Come, Giacinta. (*Taking her hand.*) Good-bye, Signor Filippo. (*Kissing him.*) Good-bye to you all. I'm your humble servant. We shall meet again in Livorno. (*He leaves.*)

VITTORIA: Till we meet again, Giacinta. Good-bye, ladies, your servant. Signor Filippo, your servant. (*Taking Guglielmo's hand.*) Let's go!

COSTANZA: Have a good journey!

ROSINA: Good journey!

SABINA: Good journey.

GUGLIELMO: (*To Vittoria, a bit peremptorily.*) All right, don't rush me. Signor Filippo, my apologies and my thanks.

FILIPPO: Good-bye. We'll see you in Livorno.

GUGLIELMO: Giacinta . . . forgive me . . .

GIACINTA: Have a good journey.

VITTORIA: (*To Guglielmo.*) What the devil's wrong? You're crying.

GUGLIELMO: (*Resolute.*) Let's go.

VITTORIA: All right! Let's go!

(*She leaves with Guglielmo.*)

FERDINANDO: Sabina . . .

SABINA: What is it?

FERDINANDO: Here, I have a present for you.

SABINA: What are you giving me?

FERDINANDO: A marriage contract.

SABINA: For me? That's not mine.

FERDINANDO: No, it's not really for you . . . because in yours there has to be a settlement!

SABINA: Look here now, you are being insolent, and I'm fed up! You've had all you're going to get from me. You should be satisfied with that. Ingrate! Blood-sucking leech! Greedy guts! (*She leaves.*)

FERDINANDO: The old lady is angry. The settlement has gone up in smoke, and for me the comedy is finished. (*He leaves.*)

COSTANZA: Giacinta, we'll get out of your way.

GIACINTA: You're going?

FILIPPO: Don't you want to play a hand or two?

COSTANZA: I must get home.

GIACINTA: As you think best.

COSTANZA: (*To Rosina.*) Get Tognino and let's go.

ROSINA: (*To Giacinta.*) Your humble servant. Excuse us.

(*She leaves with Tognino.*)

FILIPPO: Here, I'll walk you home.

COSTANZA: You're very kind. I feel so much safer with a man. (*She leaves.*)

FILIPPO: (*To Giacinta.*) I may stay and play a game of bazzica with the idiot boy. (*He goes.*)

GIACINTA: Thank heaven, I'm alone. I can let go now and confess my weakness.—Kind ladies and gentlemen, here our playwright, with all the imagination at his command, had planned a long and touching speech for a woman torn between honor and fierce passion. Imagine the heroics and the tender sentiment as she reproaches herself for not guarding her heart as well as she should, then finding excuses in accidents and unforeseen events and even her dear vacationing in the country. I thought it best to leave it out and spare you the tedium. Our comedy may not seem to be finished; but it's over as far as these *Adventures in the Country* are concerned. If something remains to be cleared up, that will perhaps be matter for a third comedy we shall in good time have the honor to play for you, thanking you now for your most indulgent reception of the two we have so far presented.

Villeggiatura

Part Three: Back from the Country

Continuing Characters from CRAZY FOR THE COUNTRY,
and ADVENTURES IN THE COUNTRY

LEONARDO
FULGENZIO
VITTORIA
CECCO
FERDINANDO
FILIPPO
GUGLIELMO
GIACINTA
BRIGIDA
TITA
A SERVANT TO FILIPPO
COSTANZA
ROSINA
TOGNINO

New Characters of BACK FROM THE COUNTRY

(*in order of speaking*)

BERNARDINO
uncle of Leonardo

PASQUALE
servant to Bernardino

TIME: *Late Autumn 1761.*
PLACE: *Livorno, a room in Leonardo's house and a room in Filippo's, as in the first comedy, plus a room in Bernardino's house and a room in Costanza's.*

Scene 1

Livorno. A room in Leonardo's house. Morning of a rainy day.
Leonardo stands at the window looking out at the rain as he sips a cup
of chocolate.

(Cecco enters and stands at the door. After a moment he clears his throat.)

LEONARDO: What is it?

CECCO: Someone to see you.

LEONARDO: Who?

CECCO: A young man with a bill. I think he's the druggist's apprentice.

LEONARDO: Why didn't you tell him I'm not in?

CECCO: I told him that yesterday and the day before, as you ordered. He's been here three or four times each day. Better see him and get rid of him.

LEONARDO: Tell him Paolino has instructions to pay the bill. Tell him he's expected in from Montenero any minute; and as soon as he arrives, the bill will be paid.

CECCO: There's also the candle-maker's bill.

LEONARDO: You ass, why don't you say I'm not home!

CECCO: I went through the whole routine: "I'll see if he's in. I'm not sure whether he is or not." And he said, "If he's not, I have orders to wait here till he returns." Here's his bill.

LEONARDO: (*Tearing it up.*) Damn his bill.

CECCO: Right.

LEONARDO: Well . . . you can go, if that's all. It is, isn't it?

CECCO: No, there's something else.

LEONARDO: What?

CECCO: Here it is. A summons.

LEONARDO: I know nothing about summonses. I don't accept summonses. Let them send it to my lawyer.

CECCO: Your lawyer is out of town.

LEONARDO: Where did he go?

CECCO: To the country.

LEONARDO: My lawyer's in the country? He packs up and leaves his clients in the lurch while he lolls around the country? I pay him! I give him his fees! I put off everybody in order to pay him for getting me out of these scrapes, and when I need him he's in the country? Is this summons addressed to me? Who brought it?

CECCO: A bailiff. He took down my name and cleared out.

LEONARDO: I don't know what I can do about it. He'll have to wait till my lawyer comes back. Always trouble of some kind—summonses, subpoenas. But as heaven is just, I don't have the money! They torment me for money I do not have! Let them be patient for a little while and I'll pay them! If I could pay them now, I would!

CECCO: On the stairs I met Signor Filippo's servant. He came to inform you and your sister that they have returned to Livorno.

LEONARDO: Good! Bring him in.

CECCO: He's left already. He had a list of thirty-seven other houses where he had to announce their return.

LEONARDO: Hmph. Bring me my hat and sword.

CECCO: Hat and sword. Right. (*He brings them to Leonardo.*) Here you are.

LEONARDO: See if there's anybody outside.

CECCO: (*Peeking out the door.*) There are two creditors still waiting.

LEONARDO: For me? Do they know I'm here?

CECCO: They know. Berto told them.

LEONARDO: Who are these two?

CECCO: Your tailor and the bootmaker.

LEONARDO: Get rid of them.

CECCO: What will I tell them?

LEONARDO: Anything you like.

CECCO: Couldn't you give them something on account?

LEONARDO: Send them away, I tell you!

CECCO: They won't go. They'll stay here till dark.

LEONARDO: Do you have the key for the secret door?

CECCO: It's over the doorframe.

LEONARDO: Good. I'll go out that way.

CECCO: Watch out for the steps. They're dark and dangerous.

LEONARDO: It doesn't matter. I have to go out.

CECCO: It's full of cobwebs too. They'll cling to your clothes.

LEONARDO: I don't care.

CECCO: Shall I just let them wait out there?

LEONARDO: Yes, let them wait till the devil comes to get them. (*He leaves.*)

(*Cecco picks up the chocolate cup and puts it on a tray.*)

(*Vittoria enters.*)

VITTORIA: Where is my brother?

CECCO: (*In a hushed voice.*) He's gone out.

VITTORIA: Why are you whispering?

CECCO: So they can't hear me outside the door.

VITTORIA: It they're right out there, they must have seen him leave.

CECCO: No, he sneaked out through the secret door.

VITTORIA: That's foolish! And bad manners, too! He has visitors waiting and he leaves without seeing them? Without even saying hello and good-bye? If they are respectable, I'll see them myself.

CECCO: You want me to bring them in?

VITTORIA: Yes. Who are they?

CECCO: The tailor and the bootmaker.

VITTORIA: What are they doing here?

CECCO: They're after their money.

VITTORIA: Why doesn't my brother pay them?

CECCO: I'm afraid he can't.

VITTORIA: Oh. Well, take care you don't tell anyone. People mustn't know. See if you can get these tradesmen to leave without a fuss. We don't want the neighbors to hear. My brother simply must understand you have to pay!

CECCO: Yes. Well put.

VITTORIA: Where did he go?

CECCO: To visit his fiancée.

VITTORIA: Oh, is Giacinta back in town?

CECCO: I believe she is.

VITTORIA: When did she return?

CECCO: This morning.

VITTORIA: (*Miffed.*) And she sent no word to me?

CECCO: Yes, she sent a servant to inform you and the master that she was back.

VITTORIA: Why didn't you tell me?

CECCO: I have been run ragged this morning. If you knew what a to-do there has been . . .

VITTORIA: I wondered. I didn't think she'd dare snub me.

CECCO: Excuse me. I hear a ruckus outside.

VITTORIA: Throw them out, the scum.

CECCO: (*Muttering.*) That's right—working people are scum.

VITTORIA: What do you mean?

(But Cecco is gone.)

(Loud voices from outside.)

(Then Cecco comes back.)

CECCO: Signor Fulgenzio is here. He asked for the master. I told him he was out, and he said he'd wait.

VITTORIA: Bring him in here. Are the creditors gone?

CECCO: Signor Fulgenzio is talking to them. *(He goes out again.)*

(We hear voices, more subdued, then silence.)

(Fulgenzio enters.)

FULGENZIO: What a mess!

VITTORIA: Ah, Signor Fulgenzio . . .

FULGENZIO: Your servant, Vittoria.

VITTORIA: . . . what ever prompted you to write that our uncle was dying? We nearly broke our necks getting back to Livorno.

FULGENZIO: I don't know what you're talking about. I never wrote you. Your uncle is in the best of health, the old scoundrel.

VITTORIA: I saw your letter to my brother.

FULGENZIO: What letter?

VITTORIA: The one you wrote!

FULGENZIO: To your brother?

VITTORIA: Yes, to my brother?

FULGENZIO: I'm afraid you've been dreaming.

VITTORIA: Dreaming? We raced to get here before our uncle died!

FULGENZIO: Who told you this nonsense?

VITTORIA: Your letter!

FULGENZIO: (*Losing his temper.*) Now don't make me mad. I tell you I wrote no letter. I wouldn't and I didn't.

VITTORIA: Then what's this all about?

FULGENZIO: Somebody's playing a trick. It's a joke, or a fabrication.

VITTORIA: Whose fabrication?

FULGENZIO: Your brother's, probably.

VITTORIA: Leonardo?

FULGENZIO: Yes. He's in hot water. They told me he owed money, but I didn't realize it was so much. I'm sorry I ever got into this business of arranging a marriage for him with Filippo's daughter. I wanted to help him out, but he's not worth it.

VITTORIA: Thank you for the testimonial. I see you want to ruin my brother.

FULGENZIO: Leonardo has ruined himself, and now he's ruining the people who gave him credit.

VITTORIA: If you really wanted to help, you would rid us of these insolent creditors.

FULGENZIO: I have. They're gone, thanks to me. I didn't guarantee they would be paid—I'm not that crazy—but I talked them out of having him arrested. If you don't pay them what you owe, at least don't call them insolent. Your brother was the insolent one when he took what he wanted from them and never paid for it. Now they have to come five, six, seven times to beg for what belongs to them. They lose whole days trying to get their rightful pay—while the brother absconds and the sister insults them. There's insolence, there's injustice, there's ingratitude for you.

VITTORIA: Lectures don't help a bit.

FULGENZIO: Yes, I see that. I'm preaching to the deaf.

VITTORIA: Preach to my brother. He is the one who needs it.

FULGENZIO: Where is your brother?

VITTORIA: He's gone to see Giacinta.

FULGENZIO: Are they back? I'm glad.

VITTORIA: I advise you not to go there and make a fuss. It's none of your business.

FULGENZIO: I'll do what I think best.

VITTORIA: Well, don't try to break a marriage contract because it shouldn't be done.

FULGENZIO: You know what shouldn't be done, young lady? Spending more than you can afford, going into debt for your entertainment, putting off your creditors and calling them names. That's what shouldn't be done.

VITTORIA: Well, that's a nice thing to say.

FERDINANDO: (*Offstage.*) Yoo-hoo! Anyone here?

VITTORIA: Oh, it's Ferdinando. (*Calling.*) Come on in! I'm here!

(Ferdinando enters.)

FERDINANDO: I bow and pay my respects.

VITTORIA: Your servant. (*Fulgenzio bows frostily and leaves.*) Welcome home.

FERDINANDO: Much obliged. I didn't expect to be back so soon.

VITTORIA: You must have come with Signor Filippo and Giacinta.

FERDINANDO: Yes, and if the trip had lasted two hours longer I might not have survived.

VITTORIA: Why not?

FERDINANDO: Because Giacinta did nothing but sigh, Signor Filippo slept soundly from Montenero to Livorno, the maid cried all the way, and I was bored to death.

VITTORIA: What was Giacinta sighing about?

FERDINANDO: Oh . . . crazy ideas she has. I was embarrassed for her.

VITTORIA: What crazy ideas?

FERDINANDO: Let's not even talk about it. Have you heard the news?

VITTORIA: About what?

FERDINANDO: Tognino.

VITTORIA: The doctor's son?

FERDINANDO: Yes. The father came back from Maremma and discovered his son wants to marry that silly girl Rosina. He chased the boy out of the house, and Tognino didn't know where he was going to eat or sleep. Costanza would like to see her niece married but she doesn't intend to spend any money on her. Finally she had to take the boy in and let him sleep with the footman. But Tognino is eating her out of house and home, so today they're bringing the boy to Livorno, suing his father for support, marrying Tognino to Rosina, and then enrolling him at the university . . . if they will take the feebleminded.

VITTORIA: It's an enchanting story, but I'm not interested. I'd rather hear about Giacinta and her crazy ideas.

FERDINANDO: Forgive me, but I make it a rule not to gossip.

VITTORIA: You've aroused my suspicions. Now you're obliged to confirm them.

FERDINANDO: Suspicions about what?

VITTORIA: The same thing I suspected at Montenero.

FERDINANDO: I don't know what that was or what you suspect now.

VITTORIA: If Giacinta is sighing, something must be bothering her.

FERDINANDO: Naturally.

VITTORIA: And it's not for my brother she's sighing.

FERDINANDO: I never thought for a minute she was.

VITTORIA: Then who is it?

FERDINANDO: Who knows? Couldn't she be sighing for me? *(He laughs.)*

VITTORIA: Oh no. Not for you, no. She's sighing for somebody else.

FERDINANDO: Speaking of that, I have lost the joy of my life. Sabina doesn't love me any more. After I brought up the subject of a settlement, she took offense and didn't ever want to see me again. You'll laugh—she wouldn't even return to Livorno for fear she would have to travel with me. She stayed on at Montenero, and I believe she is now so ashamed of her girlish behavior she doesn't want to come back. She thinks everybody here will be laughing at her.

VITTORIA: You can be proud of yourself.

FERDINANDO: I only intended to amuse the company.

VITTORIA: You certainly succeeded.

FERDINANDO: I don't see why I should be criticized for that. It's not nearly as bad as courting two girls at the same time and pretending to love one to cover up a passion for the other.

VITTORIA: What does that mean?

FERDINANDO: Whatever you want it to mean.

VITTORIA: That's horrible. That's poisonous. That wounds me to the heart.

FERDINANDO: What does it have to do with you?

VITTORIA: So that's why Giacinta was sighing?

FERDINANDO: Ask her about that.

VITTORIA: And who is courting two girls?

FERDINANDO: Ask him.

VITTORIA: What "him" are you accusing?

FERDINANDO: The accusative "him." Nominative "he," accusative "him." You seem to be in a bad humor this morning. My respects. I'm off to the coffee shop where the curious are gathered to hear all about our adventures in the country. I have enough stories to last two weeks at least. I hope to keep all Livorno laughing. Your servant. (*He leaves.*)

Scene 2

The room in Filippo's house.
Brigida and Giacinta.

BRIGIDA: Now, now. Don't think so much. Amuse yourself. Have a good time. Remember (*Indicating Giacinta's head.*) melancholy plays a lot of havoc up here.

GIACINTA: I'm not melancholy now. I'm perfectly happy. I have never felt better in my life. I wouldn't change places with a queen. I feel new born now that I don't see him any more.

BRIGIDA: Pardon me for asking—but which one do you mean by him?

GIACINTA: Guglielmo, of course!

BRIGIDA: I thought for a minute you might mean your fiancé.

GIACINTA: I have every reason to loathe Guglielmo. Could he possibly have behaved worse than he did? Humiliating me? Making me fall so madly in love with him? How miserable I've been because of him! The heartaches he gave me! The fears! I haven't had an hour's peace. Ever since the first day he began his insidious attacks, ah! how cunningly he insinuated himself into my heart! What wonderful words! What long languishing looks! What studied attentions! And how cleverly he found chances to be alone with me, and what velvet phrases he invented, and how melodiously he murmured them!

BRIGIDA: Yes . . . you never think about him, I see.

GIACINTA: Never again. Enough is enough. Thank heaven I'm free of him now. I feel as though I had been through a terrible illness . . . and now I'm completely cured!

BRIGIDA: Excuse me, but I think there is still some convalescing to do.

GIACINTA: No, you're wrong. I'm well . . . perfectly well again, just as I was before. Now all my thoughts are on preparations for my wedding. I've already decided on what gift I want from my father. And I absolutely will not have Leonardo consulting his sister about anything, especially the wedding dresses. It's not proper; she's only a girl, and she has bad taste. I'm sure she'd choose something hideous. Those are the thoughts that occupy me at present. I have nothing on my mind but dresses, jewels, Flemish lace and silk lace, and shoes, and fans . . . That is what I'm concentrating on. I don't have time for anything else.

BRIGIDA: There never passes through your mind a loving thought of your fiancé?

GIACINTA: I hope to love him some day, quite tenderly. I've heard that many who marry for love are soon bored.

BRIGIDA: Then you'll never be bored.

GIACINTA: But those who marry out of duty or simple resignation, fall in love in time and are happy together till they die.

BRIGIDA: Pray heaven that's so.

GIACINTA: That's how it has to be . . . and it will be. I'm taking Leonardo as a husband chosen for me by heaven . . . and my father, of course. I know I must respect him and love him. Respect is my duty, and as for love—well, I'll do my best.

BRIGIDA: When you promise to respect him, it means you do everything he wants.

GIACINTA: Oh, of course. But respect works both ways. If I respect him, he must also respect me and do everything I want. And he must not mistreat me or make a slave of me.

BRIGIDA: He may not see it that way.

GIACINTA: Can you imagine? That brash Guglielmo hasn't even tried to call on me.

BRIGIDA: If he did, I expect you wouldn't see him. Would you?

GIACINTA: Why shouldn't I? I'm not afraid of him. I'm completely in control. I can see him and treat him with absolute indifference. I've been weak, it's true; but in the three days since I last saw him, I've had time to think it over and strengthen my spirit and my heart. I must get used to being with him, just as I am with others. He's going to marry my sister-in-law, so now and then we'll be thrown together. What would people say if I ran away from him? No, no. I intend to begin right now getting used to seeing him, being near him . . . as if I had never loved him or even known him. And I can do it. I'm not afraid of him. You'll see yourself how bravely I carry it off.

BRIGIDA: What if your husband forbids you to see him?

GIACINTA: Leonardo would be a fool to do that. Why should he forbid me to see his brother-in-law?

BRIGIDA: You know how insidious jealousy is.

GIACINTA: Jealousy is something I will not tolerate, and Leonardo knows it.

BRIGIDA: But you'll admit he has some grounds for it.

GIACINTA: That's all over. He's had the satisfaction of Guglielmo's promise to marry Vittoria. He will marry her, and that ought to be enough. After all, Guglielmo is an honorable young man, and I am an honorable woman, and it would be outrageous to think otherwise.

(The Servant enters.)

SERVANT: Signor Guglielmo would like to pay his respects.

(Pause.)

BRIGIDA: Be brave—remember?

GIACINTA: Yes. (*To the Servant.*) Tell him to come in. He is welcome. (*The Servant goes.*) Why do you say, "Be brave"? Are you suggesting I'm afraid? Afraid of what? Don't be impertinent . . . —Oh, Brigida, an unforeseen attack of the vapors obliges me to retire! I believe it's going to my stomach! You receive Signor Guglielmo and ask him to excuse . . . —Oh, I'm going to kill myself with my bare hands! (*She rushes out.*)

(Guglielmo enters.)

GUGLIELMO: Where is your mistress?

BRIGIDA: Your pardon. She asked me to make her apologies.

GUGLIELMO: The servant told me she was here.

BRIGIDA: She was, but her father sent for her.

GUGLIELMO: I'll wait till she's at leisure.

BRIGIDA: Excuse me, but what do you want of her, please?

GUGLIELMO: Do I have to explain everything to you? I wish to pay my respects and congratulate her on her safe return. That is what I want, and that should satisfy your curiosity.

BRIGIDA: Very well. I shall convey your compliments to my mistress, and it will be as if she had received them in person.

GUGLIELMO: I'm not allowed to see her?

BRIGIDA: Later there will be plenty of time for that. She's still tired from the journey.

GUGLIELMO: This is insulting. As a man of honor, I resent it.

BRIGIDA: Of course you must take it as you please. I don't know what else I can tell you.

GUGLIELMO: Remind your mistress that I am engaged to Vittoria . . .

BRIGIDA: I believe she'll remember that without my reminding her.

GUGLIELMO: . . . and if I weren't, I should never have come here and bothered her.

BRIGIDA: As her future brother-in-law you will be seeing her quite often. You can remind her of anything you like.

GUGLIELMO: You refuse to give her a message?

BRIGIDA: With your kind indulgence, I do. I am not employed as a messenger.

GUGLIELMO: Is her father at home?

BRIGIDA: I don't know.

GUGLIELMO: You don't know? You just told me he sent for her.

BRIGIDA: If I said that, why do you ask me if he's here?

GUGLIELMO: Frankly, you strike me as very peculiar.

BRIGIDA: Your pardon. I was thinking exactly the same thing about you.

(*Leonardo enters. He sees Guglielmo and without greeting him turns to Brigida.*)

LEONARDO: Where is your mistress?

BRIGIDA: In there. With her father.

GUGLIELMO: (*To Leonardo.*) My dear friend . . .

LEONARDO: (*Distantly to Guglielmo.*) Your servant. (*To Brigida.*) Ask her if I may see her.

BRIGIDA: Of course, right away. Excuse me—is Paolino back from the country?

LEONARDO: No, not yet.

BRIGIDA: Forgive me, but when will he return?

LEONARDO: Are you going or not?

BRIGIDA: I'm going, I'm going. (*She leaves.*)

LEONARDO: You are very solicitous in coming to greet my fiancée.

GUGLIELMO: Merely paying my respects.

LEONARDO: But you are not nearly so attentive to your own fiancée.

GUGLIELMO: Please instruct me where I have been lacking.

LEONARDO: Don't make me spell it out.

GUGLIELMO: If you don't at least say it, I cannot fathom what you mean.

LEONARDO: Have you seen Giacinta?

GUGLIELMO: No. I wished to pay my respects, but I have not yet been admitted. You, however, will not be denied access; so I beg you to use your influence to permit me to render her my humble duty.

LEONARDO: Signor Guglielmo, when do you plan to marry my sister Vittoria?

GUGLIELMO: My dear friend, a marriage between two civilized persons should be solemnized with proper ceremony.

LEONARDO: But in the meantime why postpone the signing of the marriage contract?

GUGLIELMO: That can be done any time you like.

LEONARDO: Then do it today.

GUGLIELMO: Very well.

LEONARDO: Please go to the notary and tell him we are ready.

GUGLIELMO: Very well, I shall go and alert him.

LEONARDO: You'd better go at once if you expect to find him in.

GUGLIELMO: Yes, I'll go at once. I beg you to convey my humblest respects. Please tell her I came to pay my homage. (*He leaves.*)

(*Brigida, returning, watches Guglielmo's departure.*)

LEONARDO: I don't understand that man.

BRIGIDA: My mistress sends her respects and thanks you for your attentions. She regrets she cannot see you this morning because she is not feeling well and must rest.

LEONARDO: Is she in bed?

BRIGIDA: Not actually in bed, no. She's lying on the sofa. She has a splitting headache and can't bear even to talk.

LEONARDO: And I'm not permitted to see her? To pay my respects, and hear from her own mouth how she feels?

BRIGIDA: That's what she said to me, and that's what she asked me to tell you.

LEONARDO: (*Indignantly.*) Very well. Tell her I'm sorry she is ill and that I understand the reason only too well, and that for my part I shall do everything I can to restore her health at the earliest possible moment.

BRIGIDA: You mustn't think . . .

LEONARDO: (*Overriding her.*) Go and tell her what I said. (*Brigida leaves.*)

(*Leonardo remains alone and motionless, unable to make up his mind to go. Then abruptly he goes to the door of Giacinta's room. He's about to open it and go in, but he stops, drops his hand from the doorknob, and moves sadly away. He stands still for a moment.*)

(*The outer door opens and Cecco appears in a mantle, wet umbrella in hand.*)

LEONARDO: (*To himself.*) I deserve this. I deserve even worse.

CECCO: (*Sensing Leonardo's mood.*) They brought this letter for you.

LEONARDO: Thank you. (*He opens it automatically and reads. Gradually his expression changes. He reads more anxiously and then stops, the letter still in his hands, thunderstruck.*) What's this? What's this Paolino writes me? My property in the country seized . . . the furniture confiscated . . . even the linens and silverware I had rented? And Paolino himself arrested . . . (*He paces for a moment, desperate, looking around.*) I'm ruined. My reputation's gone. This finishes me. And Giacinta . . . (*He looks at her door, makes a gesture of hopelessness, looks again at the letter and goes to the window, murmuring:*) We're done for . . . done for . . .

(*A pause. Leonardo drops into a chair near the window. Cecco picks up the hat he had left by the door and looks questioningly at his master.*)

(*Through the open door comes Fulgenzio, also in mantle with wet umbrella. He sees Leonardo and stops on the threshold.*)

FULGENZIO: Here he is—the madman, the prodigal, the infatuated spendthrift. (*He comes down a few steps and, smiling ironically, he stops in front of Leonardo. Cecco, embarrassed, edges toward the door.*) So, did you have a good time in the country?

LEONARDO: (*Looking up.*) That's all, Cecco. (*Cecco leaves.*) Don't talk to me about the country. I never want to see it again.

FULGENZIO: You should have come to that decision a long time ago.

LEONARDO: Better late than never.

FULGENZIO: (*Heatedly.*) It's much too late. What more can go wrong? Are you trying to sell me fireflies as lanterns? I'm amazed that you had the nerve to involve an honest man in promoting your marriage schemes. You knew your own situation. You committed fraud, pure and simple. But I intend to let Signor Filippo know the truth. You do what you like. I wash my hands of it. I'm through with the whole mess.

LEONARDO: Signor Fulgenzio, for the love of heaven don't drive me to the last desperation. Since you know my plight, have pity on me. There's no corner I can hope to hide in. Help me, Signor Fulgenzio. I'm on the brink of the precipice; and if I fall, so will all my family.

FULGENZIO: If you were my son, I'd break my cane over your backside. It's the same old song: "I'm desperate; I want to hang myself; I want to jump in the river." I shouldn't care because you're none of mine. You deserve to be abandoned, but I haven't the heart for it.

LEONARDO: Heaven will bless you! Save me and you save a whole family from disgrace!

FULGENZIO: Save you? You think I'll ruin myself to pay your debts so you can make more?

LEONARDO: No, Signor Fulgenzio, I'll never do it again.

FULGENZIO: I don't believe you for a second.

LEONARDO: Then what did you mean when you just said . . .

FULGENZIO: I was talking about going to your Uncle Bernardino on your behalf. He is better able than I am to help you, and he has a family obligation to do it. If I take the time and the trouble to go see him with you, I'm doing more than you have the right to expect from me.

LEONARDO: I leave it to your judgment, but I'm afraid my Uncle Bernardino won't lift a finger.

FULGENZIO: Why not?

LEONARDO: Because he's mean and miserly and wouldn't give me rope to hang myself. Besides, he's so offensive I can't stand him.

FULGENZIO: May be, but it must be done. To get anywhere you have to take the first step. If your uncle won't help you, who will?

LEONARDO: That's true, I can't deny it. Everything you say is true.

FULGENZIO: Then come along.

LEONARDO: Yes, I'm coming . . . but I dread it.

(They leave.)

Scene 3

A room in Bernardino's house.
Bernardino, in an old-fashioned bathrobe, and Pasquale, his serving-man.

BERNARDINO: Who? Who is asking for me?

PASQUALE: Signor Fulgenzio. He wishes to pay his respects.

BERNARDINO: He's welcome, he's welcome. Let Signor Fulgenzio come in. He's welcome.

(Pasquale ushers in Fulgenzio.)

FULGENZIO: My regards to Signor Bernardino.

BERNARDINO: Good morning, my dear friend. How are you doing? Are you well? It's been a long time since I saw you.

FULGENZIO: I thank heaven I'm well as can be for a man getting on in years . . . and beginning to feel the aches and pains.

BERNARDINO: Do what I do: pay them no attention. Some suffering we have to put up with; but if you ignore it, you feel it less. I eat when I'm hungry; I sleep when I'm tired; I amuse myself when I'm in the mood. And I ignore everything else. Why should I bother? (*Laughing.*) It makes no difference one way or the other. And nobody cares. So I pay no attention

FULGENZIO: Heaven bless you, you have a wonderful attitude. Happy the man who can take things as you do.

BERNARDINO: (*Laughing.*) Why bother? Who cares?

FULGENZIO: I've come to you about a matter of some importance.

BERNARDINO: Dear Signor Fulgenzio, here I am! At your service!

FULGENZIO: Friend, I have to talk to you about your nephew Leonardo.

BERNARDINO: The young prince? How is the young prince? What's the young prince doing these days?

FULGENZIO: To be frank, he hasn't been very wise.

BERNARDINO: Not been very wise? It seems to me he's wiser than you and I. We work hard to make a living, while he enjoys himself, splurges, squanders his money, lives a life of luxury—and you think he's not wise?

FULGENZIO: I understand your sarcasm and how you despise such behavior.

BERNARDINO: Oh, I wouldn't dare criticize young prince Leonardo. I have too much respect for the illustrious prince, for his cleverness and his gorgeous showy clothes.

FULGENZIO: Dear friend, please let's talk seriously for a moment.

BERNARDINO: Yes, good. Let's be serious.

FULGENZIO: Your nephew is ruined.

BERNARDINO: Ruined? (*Laughing.*) You mean he's down to his last million?

FULGENZIO: You laugh and there's nothing to laugh about. Your nephew has so many debts that he doesn't know where to turn.

BERNARDINO: Is that all? He has nothing to worry about. His debts won't bother him; they'll bother his creditors.

FULGENZIO: And if he has no more credit, how will he live?

BERNARDINO: That's easy, easy. He can go have dinner one by one with the people who have eaten off him. He won't go hungry.

FULGENZIO: You refuse to take this seriously. You're mocking me.

BERNARDINO: Dear Signor Fulgenzio, you know my friendship and esteem for you!

FULGENZIO: If that is true, then listen to me and answer me civilly. You must know already that Leonardo has an opportunity to marry into a lot of money.

BERNARDINO: Wonderful.

FULGENZIO: There will be a dowry of eight thousand crowns.

BERNARDINO: Delightful.

FULGENZIO: But unless his finances can be shored up, he'll lose both the girl and the dowry.

BERNARDINO: A prince like him? All he has to do is stamp his foot and money will spurt out of the ground!

FULGENZIO: I'm losing patience. I tell you your nephew is ruined.

BERNARDINO: (*Feigning seriousness.*) He is, eh? If you say so, it must be so.

FULGENZIO: But he can easily be put right back on his feet again.

BERNARDINO: That's good.

FULGENZIO: Only he'll need your help.

BERNARDINO: Oh, that's impossible!

FULGENZIO: He's depending on you.

BERNARDINO: Come on! The young prince? Impossible!

FULGENZIO: He is, I tell you. He's counting on your generosity and your affection. If he weren't afraid of how you would receive him, he would ask in person for your blessing and your pardon.

BERNARDINO: Ask my pardon? My pardon for what? What has he done to ask my pardon for? Eh? You're joking. I don't deserve such elaborate politeness. We're relatives, Signor Leonardo and I; we're relaxed with each other. No, Signor Leonardo must pardon *me*. He shouldn't use such ceremony with me.

FULGENZIO: If he comes to you, will you receive him in friendship?

BERNARDINO: Why shouldn't I?

FULGENZIO: If you'll allow me then, I'll bring him to you.

BERNARDINO: He's welcome, whenever he wishes. He's welcome.

FULGENZIO: If you mean that, I'll call him in.

BERNARDINO: Where is Signor Leonardo?

FULGENZIO: He's in the hall, waiting.

BERNARDINO: (*Astonished.*) Waiting? In the hall?

FULGENZIO: I'll bring him in, if you consent.

BERNARDINO: Yes, he's welcome. Bring him in.

(*Fulgenzio goes and ushers in Leonardo.*)

FULGENZIO: Here he is.

LEONARDO: Please forgive me, uncle . . .

BERNARDINO: Oh, nephew, my humblest respects. How are you? Are you feeling well? How is your dear sister; how is my dearest niece? Did you have a good time in the country? Have you returned in good health? Are things going well for you? Oh, wonderful, I'm so glad.

LEONARDO: I don't deserve to be received with such affection and courtesy, and I'm afraid your words conceal the reproofs I truly do deserve.

BERNARDINO: (*To Fulgenzio.*) What a speech, eh? What a way with words this young man has! What a lovely way of expressing himself!

FULGENZIO: Let's cut out the useless palaver. I told you—he is in extreme need of your help, and he counts on you desperately.

BERNARDINO: If I can . . . if it should ever happen that I'm able . . .

LEONARDO: (*Hat in hand.*) Ah, uncle . . . !

BERNARDINO: Put on your hat.

LEONARDO: . . . unfortunately my bad management . . .

BERNARDINO: Put your hat back on.

LEONARDO: . . . has reduced me to extreme . . .

BERNARDINO: (*Clapping Leonardo's hat on his head.*) Please!

LEONARDO: . . . and if you will be generous enough to lend me . . .

BERNARDINO: (*To Fulgenzio.*) What time is it?

FULGENZIO: Listen to him, will you?

LEONARDO: (*Taking off his hat again.*) Please, uncle! Dear uncle . . .

BERNARDINO: (*Taking off his own cap.*) Your most humble servant.

LEONARDO: . . . don't turn your back on me!

BERNARDINO: Oh, I wouldn't do anything so impolite for all the money in the world!

LEONARDO: (*Standing hat in hand.*) My only weakness has been spending too much in the country.

BERNARDINO: Permit me. (*Putting his cap back on.*) Did you have a lot of company this year? Did you enjoy yourselves?

LEONARDO: It was crazy—all of it, uncle, I confess. I see it now, and I regret it with all my heart.

BERNARDINO: So you are getting married?

LEONARDO: I expect to, and the dowry of eight thousand crowns ought to put me back on my feet. But unless you help me with some debts . . .

BERNARDINO: Yes, eight thousand crowns is nice money.

FULGENZIO: The bride is the daughter of Signor Filippo Ganganelli.

BERNARDINO: Good. I know him; he's a well-known man; goes on expensive vacations; very easy-going; has a sunny nature. A happy man. It's a fine family. I'm delighted for you.

LEONARDO: But if I don't pay at least part of what I owe . . .

BERNARDINO: Please greet Signor Filippo for me.

LEONARDO: . . . if I don't clear up my debts . . .

BERNARDINO: Tell him I congratulate him.

LEONARDO: Uncle, you're not listening to me.

BERNARDINO: Oh yes I am. I hear you are getting married and I'm happy for you.

LEONARDO: And you won't help me out?

BERNARDINO: What's the bride's name?

LEONARDO: You have the heart to abandon me?

BERNARDINO: How happy I am to hear that my big nephew is getting married!

LEONARDO: Thank you for your felicitations, and don't worry . . . I'll not bother you again.

BERNARDINO: Your most humble servant.

LEONARDO: (*To Fulgenzio.*) I told you how it would be. I've had all I can take. (*He leaves.*)

BERNARDINO: (*Calling after him.*) My deepest respects to my nephew!

FULGENZIO: (*Angrily to Bernardino.*) Your servant.

BERNARDINO: Good day, my dear Signor Fulgenzio.

FULGENZIO: If I had known, I wouldn't have bothered you.

BERNARDINO: You are always welcome, day or night, any time!

FULGENZIO: You're worse than an animal.

BERNARDINO: Good Signor Fulgenzio!

FULGENZIO: I could break your neck with my own hands. (*He leaves.*)

(*Pasquale closes the door after him and comes into the room.*)

BERNARDINO: Pasquale.

PASQUALE: Master?

BERNARDINO: Serve dinner. I'm hungry.

Scene 4

> *The room in Filippo's house.*
> *Brigida and Giacinta.*

BRIGIDA: We can't always say, "I'll do this or that," or "It has to be thus or so." Sometimes it's not in our hands.

GIACINTA: You mean I won't always get my way?

BRIGIDA: You might—and I wish you luck!—but I doubt it.

GIACINTA: I know I will. I'm absolutely certain.

BRIGIDA: What makes you so sure?

GIACINTA: Let's just say heaven is on my side. You know how upset I was? Well, I tried to distract myself by reading a book I found. It was a revelation! It's called "HOME REMEDIES FOR MENTAL DISEASE, or What to Do When You Are Losing Your Mind." Among other things I learned from this wonderful book: "When you are troubled by negative thoughts, you must try to concentrate on the positive." It says here we are like a machine. We must laugh a lot to shake the machine and keep it going. Our brain is full of tiny little cells where thousands of different thoughts are locked up and ready to pop out. Will Power can open and close these tiny cells whenever it wants to, and Reason tells Will Power to close this one and open that one. For instance, when the little box in my brain makes me think of Guglielmo, I have to switch over to Reason; and Reason tells Will Power to open up other little boxes I have up there, containing Duty thoughts and Honesty and all that. If they don't pop right out, I can float around in neutral for awhile, thinking about Clothes and Card Games and the Lottery and Food and things like that. And if Reason won't work and Will Power gets stuck, I shake the whole machine. I jump up and clap my hands and laugh a lot until the machine starts going again and the tiny little evil boxes are all closed and Reason can open up the tiny little good ones—and then I have Will Power again!

BRIGIDA: I wish I could read. I'd ask you to lend me that book.

GIACINTA: Do you have thoughts that bother you too?

BRIGIDA: I have one. It never leaves me, even when I'm asleep.

GIACINTA: Tell me what it is. Maybe I can show you which little box you have to open.

BRIGIDA: The fact is I'm hopelessly in love with Paolino. He hinted he might marry me. But now he's in Montenero looking after Signor Leonardo's property, and I don't know when he'll return.

GIACINTA: Oh, that's not so bad, Brigida. I don't see any obstacle to your marriage. All you have to do is laugh a lot and open the little box of Love without closing the little box of Hope.

BRIGIDA: Both boxes are wide open.

(Enter the Servant.)

SERVANT: Visitors have come to pay their respects—Signor Leonardo's sister Vittoria, Signor Ferdinando, and Signor Guglielmo.

GIACINTA: Oh my! Tell them to come in. They're welcome.

(*The Servant goes out.*)

BRIGIDA: Here's your chance to try out the book and see if it works.

GIACINTA: Yes, I'm glad of the opportunity.

BRIGIDA: Just do what the book says.

GIACINTA: I already did. This very minute an evil thought about Guglielmo popped out and I put it away by thinking instead about Ferdinando. He's so funny he makes me laugh.

BRIGIDA: That's right. Laugh a lot and shake the machine. Then you'll be fine.

(*Enter Vittoria, Guglielmo and Ferdinando.*)

(*The Servant takes their wet umbrellas.*)

VITTORIA: Welcome home, my dear Giacinta.

GIACINTA: (*Laughing loudly.*) How good to see you! Make yourselves at home! Do sit down!

FERDINANDO: Are you feeling all right?

GIACINTA: (*Laughing even louder.*) Wonderful! I've never been better!

GUGLIELMO: I'm happy to hear it.

GIACINTA: Oh thank you! (*Grabbing a chair forcefully.*) Here! Sit down!

BRIGIDA: That's right—shake the machine.

GIACINTA: (*Maniacally.*) Do! Do! Do sit down! Please! What's new in Livorno?

VITTORIA: Nothing much.

GIACINTA: Ferdinando here will know! He goes everywhere and knows everything. He'll tell us all the news.

FERDINANDO: I came to town with you just this morning, remember? I haven't had time to learn all the gossip. But Guglielmo might know some.

GUGLIELMO: There is some news but I can't mention it here.

GIACINTA: (*Pounding on Ferdinando's arm.*) Then you tell us something amusing!

FERDINANDO: (*Flinching.*) I don't know what to say.

VITTORIA: Let's hear Guglielmo's big secret. He can tell us part of it at least.

GIACINTA: (*Laughing and continuing to pound on Ferdinando.*) No! You! You! You tell us! Tell us something amusing!

BRIGIDA: Now you're shaking his machine.

(*Brigida, having gathered the mantles, takes them out.*)

FERDINANDO: You're breaking my arm.

GIACINTA: You poor delicate little thing! Did I hurt you?

GUGLIELMO: Show him a little mercy.

GIACINTA: (*Gasping.*) Ferdinando is so funny! He makes me laugh so hard I lose my breath!

VITTORIA: What makes you so happy today?

GIACINTA: I have no idea! I've never felt like this before.

FERDINANDO: There must be a reason.

GUGLIELMO: Probably her approaching wedding.

GIACINTA: That's a lovely dress, Vittorina.

VITTORIA: Oh, it's nothing.

FERDINANDO: Vittoria's beginning to look like a bride too.

GIACINTA: Did you have it made this year?

VITTORIA: It's really last year's. I had it taken in.

GIACINTA: By Monsieur de la Réjouissance?

VITTORIA: Yes. He made my *mariage.*

FERDINANDO: À propos of *mariage,* ladies, when is the wedding to be?

GIACINTA: (*Pushing Ferdinando violently.*) You have a very bad habit of interrupting.

FERDINANDO: And you have it in for me this morning.

GIACINTA: Yes, I do. You mistreated that poor old aunt of mine.

FERDINANDO: What did I do to Signora Sabina?

GIACINTA: What did you do? The worst thing you could do! (*Looking at Guglielmo throughout.*) You took advantage of her and made her fall hopelessly in love with you. No man of honor should behave like that. No gentleman should court a lady, old or young, when there's no possible hope. He can only tarnish her reputation, whether she's a widow or a young girl. He should stop it. He should not follow her around and torment her with visits. It's barbarous, it's dangerous, it's cruel. (*Ferdinando turns to look at Guglielmo. Giacinta continues to Ferdinando:*) I'm talking to you! Don't turn away from me!

FERDINANDO: (*Rising.*) With your permission.

GIACINTA: Where are you going?

FERDINANDO: I'm leaving. I'm removing the torment of my visit.

GIACINTA: (*Laughing loudly.*) Don't be silly! Stay here!

VITTORIA: Poor man, you've beaten him to a pulp.

GIACINTA: (*Pushing him down forcefully.*) Sit down. I was joking. Poor Ferdinando, did I hurt you?

FERDINANDO: When jokes become violent . . .

GIACINTA: (*Joyously.*) Oh, here's my father, bless him. He's a hundred times happier than I am!

(Filippo enters.)

FILIPPO: Your servant, ladies . . . gentlemen.

VITTORIA: Welcome home.

FILIPPO: Have you come to dine with us?

VITTORIA: No, no, for me it's just a courtesy call.

FILIPPO: If you would favor us, you're more than welcome to dinner.

VITTORIA: Thank you, but I'm expecting company.

FILIPPO: How is Leonardo?

VITTORIA: He's well. Haven't you seen him?

FILIPPO: I'd like to, but he hasn't been around. Is his uncle still alive? Or did he die, poor man?

VITTORIA: Oh, he's alive, he's alive. He decided he wasn't ready to die.

FILIPPO: You see! And the doctors had given him up. Well, I'm glad. Tell Leonardo I'd like to talk to him about his marriage to my daughter.

VITTORIA: I'll tell him.

GUGLIELMO: Leonardo is not very solicitous. Giacinta deserves more considerate treatment.

169

(*Giacinta wipes her brow with her handkerchief.*)

FILIPPO: Well, it's dinner time.

GIACINTA: Yes, true . . .

VITTORIA: (*Rising.*) Giacinta, we'll clear out and leave you.

GIACINTA: Good-bye, Vittorina.

VITTORIA: Your servant, Signor Filippo.

FILIPPO: An honor to see you. Remember to tell Leonardo what I said.

GIACINTA: (*Irritably to Filippo.*) You repeat everything a hundred times. Do you think everybody's memory is as poor as yours?

FILIPPO: Don't snap at me.

VITTORIA: (*Leaving.*) See you soon.

GIACINTA: Good-bye.

GUGLIELMO: (*Saluting Filippo and Giacinta.*) Your servant.

FILIPPO: My respects, Guglielmo.

GUGLIELMO: (*Lingering.*) I bow to your lovely daughter.

GIACINTA: (*To Guglielmo.*) Your servant, your servant. (*To Ferdinando.*) Come back soon and make me laugh again.

FERDINANDO: (*Leaving.*) When I recover. Your servant.

FILIPPO: (*To Ferdinando.*) You're always welcome.

(*Vittoria, Ferdinando, and Guglielmo leave.*)

FILIPPO: Well, I'm going to see if dinner is ready. (*He leaves.*)

(Giacinta collapses, moaning to herself. After a moment Brigida returns.)

GIACINTA: I think I'm going out of my mind.

BRIGIDA: (*Hesitantly.*) There's something I should tell you, but I don't want to upset you.

GIACINTA: What is it?

BRIGIDA: Signor Guglielmo spoke to me, on the stairs.

GIACINTA: What did that brash fellow have to say?

BRIGIDA: If you're going to be angry, I won't say any more.

GIACINTA: I'm not angry. I'm perfectly calm. What did he say?

BRIGIDA: He had a letter.

GIACINTA: A letter?

BRIGIDA: Yes, a letter for you.

GIACINTA: For me? Were you foolish enough to take it?

BRIGIDA: No . . . No, I didn't want to take it but he tried to force it on me.

GIACINTA: Did he say anything while he was trying to force it on you?

BRIGIDA: No, nothing at all.

GIACINTA: Then how did you know he wanted to give you a letter?

BRIGIDA: He called out to me . . . and I saw the letter in his hand.

GIACINTA: How did you know it was meant for me?

BRIGIDA: He said so.

GIACINTA: Then he did talk to you.

BRIGIDA: Only a couple of words.

GIACINTA: Why did you refuse to take that letter?

BRIGIDA: Because you said he's a brash fellow. That's what you said. He's always pestering you.

GIACINTA: Why can't you ever do anything right! I'd give everything I own to see that letter.

BRIGIDA: But I . . .

GIACINTA: You always know it all, don't you? You always make decisions for other people!

BRIGIDA: Oh, I see what you're up to. You're saying that to find out if I took it.

GIACINTA: (*Sweetly.*) Brigida . . . did you take the letter?

BRIGIDA: If I had taken it, would you beat me?

GIACINTA: No, dear, I would thank you, I would bless you, I would give you a wonderful present.

BRIGIDA: (*Warily.*) You would? Really?

GIACINTA: (*More sweetly than ever.*) Brigida. Did you take it?

BRIGIDA: I thought he might give it to somebody else . . . and I'd better take it.

GIACINTA: Ah! Give it to me. Don't make me die of suspense.

BRIGIDA: Was I wrong to take it?

GIACINTA: No! Bless you for it. Let me just see it.

BRIGIDA: (*Handing it over.*) There.

GIACINTA: Heavens! My heart is fluttering; my hands are trembling. This letter could be the end of me.

BRIGIDA: Do what I do with letters . . . burn them.

GIACINTA: You can't read.

BRIGIDA: Thank God.

GIACINTA: Go away now. Leave me.

BRIGIDA: I don't think I should.

GIACINTA: (*Testily.*) Go away, I said, and don't bother me.

BRIGIDA: (*As she goes.*) There goes my wonderful present. I was afraid of that.

(She leaves. Giacinta opens the letter and reads to herself, murmuring some of the words aloud.)

GIACINTA: " . . . I have dared to write . . . to let you know I have not faltered in my devotion . . . I promise to do nothing more to trouble or upset you . . . " What a noble heart! But it's too late now. "They are saying openly that your fiancé Leonardo is completely ruined and will not be able to afford the expenses of a wedding, nor does your father want to see you married to a bankrupt." Oh heavens! "If through no fault of your own you find yourself free, allow me to say that I too am free. I have not yet signed the marriage contract with Vittoria and nothing will induce me to sign it before I actually see you married and forever lost to me. Forgive me and pity me. I remain with the greatest respect and the sincerest devotion your most humble servant— Guglielmo." (*After a beat.*) Ah, Guglielmo . . . ! Where is Reason? Where is Will Power?

Scene 5

The room in Filippo's house.
Fulgenzio, the Servant and Leonardo.

FULGENZIO: Is Signor Filippo still at dinner?

SERVANT: They have just served the fruit, so it will be only a few minutes. If you would like me to tell him . . .

FULGENZIO: No, no, let them finish eating. I know how fond he is of his food. But when Signor Filippo leaves the table, then tell him I'm here.

SERVANT: Very well.

(The Servant leaves.)

LEONARDO: I hope to heaven Signor Filippo doesn't know of my disgrace.

FULGENZIO: He returned to town only a few hours ago. He has probably heard nothing yet.

LEONARDO: I'm so ashamed I hate to face anyone. That miserly uncle of mine was the last straw.

FULGENZIO: May the canker take him!

LEONARDO: I told you what to expect from him.

FULGENZIO: I didn't believe it was possible.

LEONARDO: I went along only to please you.

FULGENZIO: We had to try, and I'm glad we did. We may have failed with the old miser, but I'm not giving up. I've taken on the job of helping you, and help you I will.

LEONARDO: It's a providence—your kind heart and your generosity.

FULGENZIO: Now we'll try again with Filippo. I trust we shall succeed; but if we shouldn't, don't you lose hope. I'll certainly not let you go under.

LEONARDO: Your plan couldn't be better, and Signor Filippo is sure to agree. What will be much more difficult is persuading Giacinta to leave Livorno.

FULGENZIO: She'll have to go if she marries you.

LEONARDO: Yes . . . Still, I'd like her to come along willingly, out of love —but I'm afraid she'll resist.

FULGENZIO: Giacinta is a little willful. Obstinate is what she is! I noticed it when she insisted on taking that young dandy Guglielmo in the carriage with her to the country. Tell me, what happened there?

LEONARDO: Don't ask. She had me worried, I'll tell you that. But Guglielmo finally gave me his word to marry my sister.

FULGENZIO: Yes, yes, I know about that. Another harvest of the countryside! If that marriage goes well, it will be a miracle. O liberation! The way women behave these days!

LEONARDO: Here comes Signor Filippo.

FULGENZIO: You can slip away if you like. Let me handle it.

LEONARDO: I'll be anxious to see how it turns out. *(Leonardo retires to the background.)*

(Filippo enters.)

FILIPPO: Well, well! My dear Fulgenzio!

FULGENZIO: Welcome home, Filippo.

FILIPPO: Good to see you again, old friend.

FULGENZIO: Did you enjoy the country?

FILIPPO: We had a wonderful time. The best of company, the best of food —excellent veal, capons that were stupendous, quail, thrush, pheasants, partridges . . . I tell you I gave some tremendous dinners.

FULGENZIO: I'm glad you enjoyed it. Now that you're back . . .

FILIPPO: And that crazy Ferdinando had us all in stitches.

FULGENZIO: Yes, in the country you always need some clown to break the monotony.

FILIPPO: He got the idea of chasing that silly old sister of mine. Listen, if that damned nitwit didn't . . .

FULGENZIO: Tell me about it when we have more time. Right now let me explain to you . . .

FILIPPO: No, no, listen, if you want a good laugh . . .

FULGENZIO: I'm not much in the mood to laugh at the moment. I need to talk seriously to you.

FILIPPO: Well . . . I am at your disposal. Talk.

FULGENZIO: Now, Filippo, since you have returned to town . . .

FILIPPO: You know the doctor at Montenero?

FULGENZIO: Yes.

FILIPPO: And that son of his—do you know him?

FULGENZIO: No, I never met the boy.

FILIPPO: What a character! A numbskull! You'd dislocate your jaw laughing at him . . . and stupid beyond belief!

FULGENZIO: We'll have time later on. I'll be delighted to hear about him then.

FILIPPO: I had to play bazzica with the fathead!

FULGENZIO: Friend, if you don't want to hear what I came for, just say so and I'll leave.

FILIPPO: What are you talking about? Of course I want to hear! Fulgenzio old friend, I'd listen if you came in the middle of the night!

FULGENZIO: To be brief—now that you're back in Livorno, have you given any thought to your daughter's marriage?

FILIPPO: It's always on my mind.

FULGENZIO: Have you seen Leonardo?

FILIPPO: No, not yet. I know he's been here, but I haven't seen him. I'm always the last in everything, so I'll be the last in that too.

FULGENZIO: From what I hear . . .

FILIPPO: At Montenero I was always the last. Every time! Even the waiters at the coffee shop would serve everybody and I would be the last!

FULGENZIO: Well now, in the business I'm talking about, you have to be the first.

FILIPPO: Oh, I know why I have to be first. Because I have to put up eight thousand crowns for the dowry.

FULGENZIO: Tell me in confidence, just between you and me: the eight thousand crowns— do you have the money on hand?

FILIPPO: To be absolutely honest with you, at the moment I couldn't put up a solitary soldo.

FULGENZIO: Then what do you intend to do?

FILIPPO: I don't know. I have some property, some buildings. Do you think I could raise the money on those?

FULGENZIO: Yes, you might. At interest, of course.

FILIPPO: Then I'll have to borrow at interest.

FULGENZIO: You'll pay almost four percent.

FILIPPO: Then I'll have to pay four percent.

FULGENZIO: Do you realize that four percent on eight thousand crowns comes to three hundred and twenty crowns at the end of the year?

FILIPPO: No! Three hundred and twenty?

FULGENZIO: And you can't get out of this marriage. The contract is drawn up and signed, and you have promised to pay the dowry.

FILIPPO: I sign and I promise because they make me sign and promise. Why didn't you tell me what it would cost when you came to me about this marriage? Forgive me, but I think I have legitimate cause to complain. If you were the good friend you say you are...

FULGENZIO: I am your friend, and if you follow my advice you can settle this amicably and honorably. I want to see your daughter married without your putting out any cash: without borrowing from anyone...and without touching the dowry.

FILIPPO: If you can do that, I'll say you've got the best business head in the world.

FULGENZIO: Do you still have that property at Genoa?

FILIPPO: Yes, there's something or other my uncle left me up there. I don't know exactly what it is. It's managed by a man who used to be my uncle's administrator. In six years he's sent me nothing from it except two baskets of macaroni.

FULGENZIO: I was in Genoa while your uncle was still alive and for some time after his death, and I know the property. Your manager is eating up the profits; and since through your own carelessness you're receiving nothing, here's what you do. Instead of the eight thousand crowns, you assign your daughter, as dowry, the property you own in Genoa. I'll see that Leonardo accepts it and is happy with it. He can go live in Genoa with his bride and manage the property in his wife's name. He won't be able to sell it or fritter it away because it will be entailed as dowry. In a nutshell, at present it brings you in nothing . . .

FILIPPO: Some macaroni.

FULGENZIO: Some macaroni! Well, for him, with a little management, it can bring in double what the eight thousand crowns would have. What do you say?

FILIPPO: Good, very good! They can have it. Let 'em go to Genoa, enjoy the profits and give me what they can; I don't care. You handle it. I turn the whole thing over to you.

FULGENZIO: That's settled then. Leave it to me.

FILIPPO: Hey, tell me, could you arrange to have Leonardo send me a basket of macaroni now and then?

FULGENZIO: He'll send whatever you want—candied fruits from Genoa . . . oranges from Portugal . . .

FILIPPO: Oh, I like oranges! And candied fruits too!

FULGENZIO: Then it's a deal?

FILIPPO: It's a deal. A good deal too.

FULGENZIO: And your daughter will be happy with it?

FILIPPO: Now, that's the problem.

FULGENZIO: Can't you tell her she'll have to do things your way?

FILIPPO: I've never made a habit of it.

FULGENZIO: This time you'll have to.

FILIPPO: I'll have to?

FULGENZIO: Everything depends on this.

FILIPPO: Depends on this? Then I'll do it. I'll do it.

FULGENZIO: When will you speak to her?

FILIPPO: This minute. I'll go right now. You wait here. (*Turning back.*) Wouldn't it be better if you did it?

FULGENZIO: Don't you want to talk to her?

FILIPPO: I'll talk to her after you do.

FULGENZIO: Go on then, bring her here if you wish.

FILIPPO: Right away. If this works and I get her off my hands, I can live like a king. (*He goes.*)

(*Leonardo comes out of hiding.*)

FULGENZIO: So far so good—if we don't run into opposition from the girl. She's headstrong, that daughter of his.

LEONARDO: Signor Fulgenzio, I think we're safe in harbor now.

FULGENZIO: Did you hear what I told him?

LEONARDO: I heard it all. I pray to heaven that Giacinta will agree.

FULGENZIO: We'll soon know. If the father doesn't act like a complete ninny, the girl will have to go along.

LEONARDO: I was thinking of something else too. What do I do about my debts here in Livorno? Do I have to sneak out of town?

FULGENZIO: I considered that. Here's what we can do. You make your bargain with Filippo and you give me power of attorney. You put your property in my hands and I act as your agent. I pay your creditors and then turn the net proceeds over to you, free of liens and legally accounted for.

LEONARDO: Heaven thank you for it! I wouldn't have the words myself.

FULGENZIO: Thank your Uncle Bernardino.

LEONARDO: Why should I thank that old skinflint?

FULGENZIO: He made me so mad I decided to help you just to spite him — at the risk of my own welfare if need be.

LEONARDO: You wouldn't do it if you didn't have a good heart.

(Filippo returns.)

FILIPPO: Have you heard the news? Oh, your servant, Leonardo.

LEONARDO: My respects, Signor Filippo.

FULGENZIO: (*To Filippo.*) What news?

FILIPPO: My daughter is not in the house. They tell me she's gone to see Costanza.

LEONARDO: Ah. I'm sorry to hear that.

FILIPPO: (*To Leonardo.*) Has Signor Fulgenzio told you . . . ?

LEONARDO: Yes, I know.

FILIPPO: Well, are you satisfied with the arrangement?

LEONARDO: I'm delighted.

FILIPPO: Good! Then we're all happy.

LEONARDO: What about Giacinta?

FILIPPO: Hmm. Let's go find her at Costanza's.

FULGENZIO: We could wait here for her to return.

LEONARDO: My sister is also going there. Perhaps they are together.

FILIPPO: It wouldn't be a bad idea for us too.

LEONARDO: That's true. We owe Costanza a visit.

FILIPPO: And we can talk to Giacinta there.

FULGENZIO: But in somebody else's house we can't speak freely.

FILIPPO: If we can't talk we'll bring her away.

LEONARDO: What do you say, Signor Fulgenzio?

FULGENZIO: Let's wait here for her. An hour one way or the other won't make any difference.

FILIPPO: (*Annoyed.*) I say we should go talk to her—immediately.

LEONARDO: (*To Filippo.*) Let's go. Let's not irritate him.

FULGENZIO: You're very obstinate, Filippo.

FILIPPO: Well, I'm a man who is used to managing things and solving problems. I know what I'm doing and I know what I'm talking about. I don't procrastinate. (*To Fulgenzio.*) You can broach the subject to her first.

(*They leave.*)

Scene 6

> *A room in Costanza's house.*
> *Costanza and Rosina.*

COSTANZA: Rosina, get yourself ready. We are going out to make some calls.

ROSINA: So soon? We just arrived.

COSTANZA: I want to visit Giacinta and then Vittoria.

ROSINA: But, auntie, we came back to Livorno after they did. It's up to them to visit us first.

COSTANZA: That's exactly what I don't want to happen. If they come here, how am I going to receive them with the house like this? There's not a decent room in the place—everything old and worn out and falling apart.

ROSINA: That's the truth. There's a big difference between this rat-trap and your pretty little cottage in the country.

COSTANZA: Of course there's a difference. I furnished the cottage for myself. This place is where my husband wallows.

ROSINA: Oh, uncle doesn't know or care. He never sees anybody but shopkeepers, and style means nothing to him.

COSTANZA: That's what I can't stand. From now on I want to spend ten months out of the year in the country. There at least I'm looked up to.

ROSINA: But the doctor there won't treat you any more.

COSTANZA: Frankly I'm sorry to lose the doctor's friendship. I made this sacrifice for your sake. I'm fond of you and I wanted to see you married, since you have no dowry and I can't give you one. If the doctor's youngster hadn't come along, I'm afraid you would have been left an old maid.

ROSINA: I'm married all right, but a lot of good it's done me. I don't have a ring or a trousseau or even a wedding dress. What are people going to say when they find out?

COSTANZA: In time you'll have all that. Meanwhile there's no need to mention your marriage. Nobody has to know. After we have made the doctor send some money to support his son, we'll announce it.

ROSINA: Then Tognino had better stop telling everybody he meets.

COSTANZA: Gag him. Where is Tognino?

ROSINA: Getting dressed up.

COSTANZA: What do you mean—getting dressed up?

ROSINA: He says that now he's in town he wants to look spiffy.

COSTANZA: What's he got to put on except those old things he wore in Montenero?

ROSINA: He brought a suit of his father's.

COSTANZA: His father is a lot bigger than he is.

ROSINA: Oh, Tognino is not so small.

COSTANZA: He must go to Pisa and start his studies at the university.

ROSINA: Not right away!

COSTANZA: Do you want him to miss a term?

ROSINA: No, but not so soon! Not for another month at least!

COSTANZA: A week or two maybe.

ROSINA: Here he is, here he is. He's all dressed up.

(Enter Tognino in a suit much too large for him, with a long perruque and a hat with a feather in the old-fashioned style.)

TOGNINO: Here I am! How do I look?

COSTANZA: (*To Rosina.*) What a spectacle! Didn't I tell you?

ROSINA: It's a little big—in spots.

COSTANZA: Go take that off this instant. You look like a poor boy at a frolic.

TOGNINO: You want me to walk around naked?

COSTANZA: Where are your old clothes?

TOGNINO: I gave them to Tita. He helped me sneak this suit out of my father's trunk.

COSTANZA: A fine exchange!

TOGNINO: It's nice. Look at the ribbons and the fringe. It may be a little long, but that doesn't matter. Doesn't it look grand on me? What do you say, Rosina?

ROSINA: It's out of style. It needs to be taken in—and let out at the crotch.

TOGNINO: Will you let me out at the crotch, auntie? And take me in?

COSTANZA: Hush up or I'll box your jaws. I'll have to thump some sense into that thick skull of yours. Don't call me auntie, and don't tell a soul you two are married.

TOGNINO: Oh, I don't talk.

ROSINA: Darling, it's time to put your *brain* to work.

TOGNINO: How do you mean?

ROSINA: By studying at the university! Learning to be a doctor!

TOGNINO: I'll study all you want as long as you give me enough to eat and take me for a walk and let me play bazzica.

COSTANZA: You poor little moron!

TOGNINO: What's a moron?

COSTANZA: If you don't have brains enough to know . . .

TOGNINO: I won't be scolded.

(Tita enters.)

TITA: Signora . . .

TOGNINO: I'm a married man! And I won't be insulted!

COSTANZA: Hush!

ROSINA: Hush!

TITA: Signor Tognino is married?

COSTANZA: He doesn't know what he's talking about. And don't you meddle in other people's business.

TITA: Beg pardon. Signora Giacinta is coming to pay her respects.

COSTANZA: Giacinta!

ROSINA: (*To Costanza.*) What can she want? We'll have to see her.

COSTANZA: Does she know we're at home?

TITA: I'm sure she does. She sent her servant ahead, and of course he knows.

COSTANZA: (*To Rosina.*) Then we'll have to see her. (*To Tita.*) Tell her she's welcome. Listen—tell her to forgive the way the place looks, that we just got home. Listen—go to the shop and get some coffee. Hey, listen!—if my husband comes home, tell him not to come in if he's in his work clothes—either get dressed in his good suit or stay in his room.

TITA: Very well. (*He goes.*)

COSTANZA: (*To Tognino.*) And you get out of here. Don't let yourself be seen in that clown suit.

TOGNINO: You're sending me out because you don't want me to have any coffee. I want some coffee.

COSTANZA: Get out before you bring on my bile and I chase you out of the house!

TOGNINO: I'm a married man!

COSTANZA: Rosina, I've had all I can take of him.

ROSINA: (*To Tognino.*) Go on, dear. You go on out and I'll bring you some coffee.

TOGNINO: I'm married. I'm a married man. (*He leaves.*)

COSTANZA: Now look here, if this goes on much longer, I won't be responsible. I absolutely refuse to put up with him.

ROSINA: Forgive him. He's still a boy.

COSTANZA: That's right—find excuses for him.

ROSINA: He's my husband; I have to find excuses. After all, I took him on your advice.

COSTANZA: Hush. Here's Giacinta.

ROSINA: He doesn't know any better. There's no use scolding him.

(*Enter Giacinta.*)

GIACINTA: Your servant, Costanza.

COSTANZA: Your most humble servant.

ROSINA: Devoted servant.

GIACINTA: My respects, Rosina.

COSTANZA: You shouldn't have taken all the trouble to come see us.

GIACINTA: No trouble at all, simply my duty.

COSTANZA: I'm terribly chagrined for you to see the house in such a mess.

GIACINTA: Oh, it looks lovely. Don't feel apologetic for my sake.

COSTANZA: When I left for the country everything went to rack and ruin. Please sit down. And excuse the chair if it's not just as it should be.

GIACINTA: It's splendid. What news of my Aunt Sabina?

ROSINA: Oh, poor Signora Sabina has been having a terrible time. I went to see her before we left and she gave me a letter for Ferdinando.

GIACINTA: Oh? I'd love to hear what she says.

ROSINA: I'm sure Ferdinando will show it to you.

COSTANZA: How is Leonardo, Giacinta?

GIACINTA: He's fine.

ROSINA: And Vittoria?

GIACINTA: Very well.

COSTANZA: And Guglielmo?

(A small pause.)

GIACINTA: Is it true that Tognino came to Livorno with you?

COSTANZA: Yes, he came . . . for a few days.

ROSINA: On his way to Pisa.

COSTANZA: To study at the university.

ROSINA: To be a doctor.

GIACINTA: Oh, of course he came through on his way to Pisa! And those ugly gossips said he was marrying Rosina.

ROSINA: They said that?

GIACINTA: I knew you would never do such a stupid thing.

ROSINA: Would it really be so stupid?

(A pause.)

COSTANZA: Tell us, will your wedding be soon?

GIACINTA: I'm not sure yet. I shall leave it up to father.

ROSINA: When is Vittoria marrying Guglielmo?

GIACINTA: (*Smiling brightly.*) You mean to tell me they're back too? So early?

COSTANZA: There's nobody left in the country. When Leonardo and Vittoria departed so suddenly, they broke up the party.

ROSINA: (*To Giacinta.*) When is Vittoria getting married?

GIACINTA: I really don't know. You'll have to ask her.

ROSINA: Perhaps you think Vittoria's marriage is stupid too.

GIACINTA: (*Rising.*) With your permission, I'll get out of your way.

COSTANZA: Oh, please stay and have some coffee.

GIACINTA: No. I'm much obliged to you.

COSTANZA: Here it comes. Please be good enough to stay.

(Tita enters with coffee.)

GIACINTA: Well. I don't want to refuse your gracious hospitality.

(*They all sit again.*)

COSTANZA: (*Handing Giacinta coffee.*) Here you are.

ROSINA: By your leave. (*She takes a cup for Tognino and gives it to Tita, who whispers to her before going out. Rosina turns at once to her aunt, explaining.*) Visitors. We have other visitors.

COSTANZA: Who is it?

ROSINA: Vittoria, Ferdinando, and Guglielmo.

(*Giacinta spills her coffee.*)

GIACINTA: Oh, what have I done?

ROSINA: Oh, look, you've spilled coffee on your *andrienne*. (*Giacinta wipes her gown with her handkerchief.*) Shall I bring some water?

GIACINTA: (*Chagrined.*) Don't bother. It doesn't matter.

ROSINA: Here they are.

(*Vittoria and Guglielmo enter.*)

VITTORIA: Your servant. How nice to see you.

COSTANZA: Servant.

ROSINA: Servant.

GUGLIELMO: Your servant.

VITTORIA: You here too, Giacinta?

GIACINTA: I also came to pay my respects.

ROSINA: You do me honor.

COSTANZA: Do sit down . . . wherever you can find a place.

GUGLIELMO: Forgive me, Costanza, if I add to your inconvenience. I met Vittoria by chance on the street and she persuaded me to come along.

ROSINA: Not at all. You favor us by coming, and for that we are indebted to Vittoria.

GIACINTA: Tell me, Vittoria, wasn't Ferdinando with you?

VITTORIA: Yes, Ferdinando had dinner with us. Guglielmo was not around and I took advantage of Ferdinando's escort.

GIACINTA: You mean he left you alone with Guglielmo?

GUGLIELMO: No, Ferdinando came with us as far as the door.

VITTORIA: (*To Guglielmo.*) She's talking to me and you are interrupting. What do you care, Giacinta, if Ferdinando came along or not?

GIACINTA: I ask because these ladies have a letter for Ferdinando from my Aunt Sabina.

ROSINA: Yes, here it is. I promised to give it to him personally.

COSTANZA: I saw him in the hall just now. What's holding him?

ROSINA: He must be somewhere in the house. I'm certainly not going to search for him.

GUGLIELMO: So Sabina has written a letter to Ferdinando.

ROSINA: Yes. I brought it for her.

GUGLIELMO: It's only right for Ferdinando to answer it.

ROSINA: He'll answer it if he wants to, I imagine.

GUGLIELMO: (*Looking at Giacinta.*) When one receives a letter it's only proper to reply.

GIACINTA: If the letter deserves an answer.

GUGLIELMO: Any letter obliges well-brought-up people to reply, especially if the letter is honest and written with sincerity and love.

GIACINTA: Love is not always lawful, and sincerity is sometimes confused with self-indulgence.

VITTORIA: Guglielmo and Giacinta seem very familiar with the contents of that letter.

GUGLIELMO: Everyone is familiar with Sabina's passion.

GIACINTA: And everyone knows it's a passion that should not be encouraged.

VITTORIA: I'd love to hear what's in that letter. Here he is; here's Ferdinando.

(Ferdinando and Tognino enter.)

FERDINANDO: Come in, Tognino my boy, my joy, my bucko.

TOGNINO: Here I am. Humble servant.

COSTANZA: (*To Tognino.*) Get out of here.

FERDINANDO: Let him stay. Show some respect for a married man.

COSTANZA: Who said he was married?

FERDINANDO: He told me so himself.

COSTANZA: There's not a word of truth in it.

FERDINANDO: (*To Tognino.*) No truth in it?

TOGNINO: (*Looking at Costanza, mortified.*) No.

FERDINANDO: No? Well then, I'm glad. If you're not going to marry Rosina, I'll court her myself. If you won't have her, I will.

(Tognino puts his index fingers to his forehead, making the gesture to indicate cuckold.)

TOGNINO: Cu cu!

FERDINANDO: Cu cu? What does this "cu cu" mean?

TOGNINO: It means that Rosina and I have been . . .

ROSINA: Hush up! Tell Ferdinando to go marry Sabina. Here's a letter she sent him.

FERDINANDO: A letter from my dear Sabina?

ROSINA: Yes. She sent it by me. I brought it this morning from Montenero.

FERDINANDO: From my darling little precious? I'll read it with all the joy in the world!

VITTORIA: We'd like to hear it too.

COSTANZA: Yes, of course. Let us all in on it.

GUGLIELMO: (*To Ferdinando.*) Just remember that letters should be answered.

GIACINTA: (*To Ferdinando.*) When they deserve an answer.

FERDINANDO: Very well. I hear you.

VITTORIA: Read it aloud so we can all enjoy it.

FERDINANDO: (*Opening the letter.*) I promise not to leave out a comma.

(Tita enters.)

TITA: Signor Filippo, Signor Leonardo, and Signor Fulgenzio ask to pay their respects.

COSTANZA: Tell them they are welcome. And bring some chairs.

TITA: I'll see what I can find. (*He leaves.*)

VITTORIA: I'm sorry for the interruption. I'd like to hear that letter. Give it here. You shan't read it without us.

(*She takes the letter from Ferdinando.*)

(*Filippo, Leonardo, and Fulgenzio enter. All rise.*)

FILIPPO: Your servant, ladies and gentlemen.

TOGNINO: Oh, you're welcome, Signor Filippo.

FILIPPO: (*To Tognino.*) Look at you! What a splendid outfit!

TOGNINO: Want to play bazzica?

FILIPPO: Not now. Giacinta, with the permission of our hostess, I'd like to have a little word with you.

COSTANZA: Please feel free.

LEONARDO: (*To Filippo.*) Excuse me, but we are here to pay our respects to Signora Costanza. You will have plenty of time to speak with Giacinta.

FILIPPO: When I have something on my mind I can't wait. Signora Costanza is good enough to understand and will forgive me.

COSTANZA: Make yourself quite at home.

GIACINTA: What is it, father?

FILIPPO: If we might go into another room, I have only a few words to say and then we can return to this delightful company.

GIACINTA: (*To Costanza.*) If you would be good enough . . .

COSTANZA: I'm so sorry. The rooms are all topsy-turvy. If you like, you can talk in the hall.

FILIPPO: Yes, yes, that's fine. Let's go, let's go. With your permission. When once I get going . . . (*He leaves.*)

GIACINTA: By your leave. I'll be right back. (*She leaves.*)

FULGENZIO: (*To Leonardo.*) Here we go. How do you feel? Hopeful?

LEONARDO: No—not very.

FULGENZIO: If she were my daughter she'd do what I say or she could go to blazes.

(*They leave.*)

TOGNINO: (*To Rosina.*) I'll go in the kitchen and listen to what they say. (*He leaves.*)

FERDINANDO: How many are in on this discussion of theirs, I wonder. I'm dying to read that letter.

VITTORIA: Read it aloud. We'll all listen. Giacinta can hear about it later.

COSTANZA: I must confess I'd like to hear it too.

ROSINA: The poor old lady was crying when she handed it to me.

FERDINANDO: Diamine! It seems to be written in Arabic!

VITTORIA: Guglielmo, are you asleep?

GUGLIELMO: No, I'm not asleep.

VITTORIA: You're all phlegm and I'm all fire.

FERDINANDO: Oh, now I'm beginning to get it!

VITTORIA: Read it all. Don't leave anything out.

FERDINANDO: With the greatest pleasure in the world. Listen: "Cruel one . . . " (*As all laugh moderately.*) "You have wounded me to the heart. You are the first who can boast of seeing me weep for love. If you knew . . . if I could tell you everything, perhaps it might make you weep in sympathy. Since you left I have not eaten, I have not drunk, I cannot sleep. I look at myself in the mirror and scarcely recognize myself. Long bouts of weeping have weakened my vision to the point where I can hardly see the paper I'm writing on. Ah! Ferdinando, my heart, my hope, my beauty . . . " (*As they all laugh again.*) Are you laughing because she calls me her beauty?

VITTORIA: The poor woman is practically blind.

ROSINA: Her eyes were always bad.

COSTANZA: They water all the time anyhow.

FERDINANDO: All right, all right! She recognizes beauty when she sees it.

(*They laugh again.*)

VITTORIA: Let's hear the rest of the letter.

FERDINANDO: You don't deserve to hear any more.

VITTORIA: Go on. We want to hear.

FERDINANDO: Where was I? Where did I leave off?

VITTORIA: Are you sleeping, Guglielmo?

GUGLIELMO: No.

FERDINANDO: Here it is. " . . . my hope, my beauty, come for pity's sake and console me. Ah yes, come, if you love me. I shall not be ungrateful; and if the heart I have given you is not enough, come, my dear, for I promise you . . . ." What the devil! She writes something here I can't make out. Her hand must have been trembling terribly. Here now—now I think I understand. "Come, my dear, for I promise you a settlement, the settlement, an ample settlement, I promise the settlement . . . " *(Once again!)* " . . . the settlement I promise with all my being. Your most faithful lover and future spouse, Sabina Borgna."

VITTORIA: Good for you!

COSTANZA: Congratulations.

ROSINA: And three cheers for the beauty of Ferdinando.

VITTORIA: What are you going to do about it?

FERDINANDO: I have made a heroic decision. I'm taking the stage coach and hastening to console my adored Sabina. Ladies and gentlemen, your most humble servant. (*He leaves.*)

VITTORIA: He goes to console himself . . . with the settlement.

COSTANZA: Poor crazy old woman!

VITTORIA: Guglielmo . . . Are you asleep?

GUGLIELMO: No, I'm not.

VITTORIA: You're not laughing at all this?

GUGLIELMO: It doesn't make me feel like laughing.

VITTORIA: Such a man!

ROSINA: Here they are. The conference is over.

(Giacinta, Filippo, Fulgenzio, and Leonardo enter. Guglielmo rises.)

VITTORIA: That seems to wake you up.

GUGLIELMO: Believe me, I wasn't asleep.

(Everyone rises.)

FILIPPO: Here we are. Excuse us, Signora Costanza.

COSTANZA: That's quite all right.

VITTORIA: Well, what news, brother of mine?

LEONARDO: Very good news, sister. Early tomorrow I'm leaving for Genoa.

VITTORIA: For Genoa?

LEONARDO: Yes.

VITTORIA: Alone?

LEONARDO: No.

VITTORIA: Who is going with you, if I may ask?

LEONARDO: Giacinta.

VITTORIA: I suppose you'll have a marriage ceremony first.

LEONARDO: Oh yes.

VITTORIA: How about us, Guglielmo?

GUGLIELMO: Giacinta is going to Genoa?

GIACINTA: Yes, I'm going to Genoa—thank heaven and my father and Signor Fulgenzio, bless him. You're all surprised that I should come to such a sudden decision. I confess that leaving the person I love more than my life . . . (*Not looking at Guglielmo's sudden move.*) I mean you, my dear father—my tender loving father! . . . leaving someone so dear tears the heart from my breast and it's a wonder I don't die of it. (*Recovering.*) But duty demands it, and obedience, and honor—they all demand it. Whoever is listening will understand. (*Turning to Leonardo.*) You, my husband, understand me—you know we could not ask for more in our present circumstances. I'll be leaving a place that has become dismal to me. I'll be leaving behind my infatuations, my anxieties, my weaknesses. I mean to forget ambition and vanity and my absurd devotion to our wonderful vacations in the country. If

I had continued on that path, who knows into what pit I might have fallen? When we change the landscape around us and the sky over our heads, we must also change our way of life. Here is my husband. Here is the man the gods have destined for me and my father has allotted me. I shall do my duty and leave others to do theirs. (*Briskly.*) Leonardo, we must leave. You have affairs to put in order, and I have many things to do. But first, let us take our vows in the presence of my father, and the mistress of this house, and these guests. I offer you my hand and ask for yours in return.

FILIPPO: (*To Fulgenzio.*) Ah! What do you say to that? It makes me cry.

LEONARDO: Yes, my dear Giacinta, if your father consents . . .

FILIPPO: I'm very happy, very happy.

LEONARDO: . . . here is my hand and my heart.

GIACINTA: Yes . . . mine too.

(*She sways.*)

LEONARDO: Heavens! You're pale! You're trembling! Is this a sign you don't love me? Tell me the truth. If there is something or someone forcing you to marry me . . .

GIACINTA: No. Nothing is forcing me. No one could do that. I decided on my own. Excuse the weakness of my sex, if modesty does not seem a virtue to you. The passage from maidenhood, single and free, to the state of marriage is a long journey in the dark, and cannot be accomplished without great struggle and commotion of spirit and thoughts. To tear out one love, one loyalty—and substitute another— to leave a . . . a father and follow a husband cannot help but agitate the heart—a heart still tender and sensitive and weakened by the cruel parting. Reason is no help at a time like this. Only Will Power. Here is my hand; I am your wife.

(*She gives Leonardo her hand.*)

LEONARDO: Yes, my dear one. I am yours; you are mine.

(He takes Giacinta's hand.)

(Tognino enters.)

TOGNINO: Weddings, weddings, weddings! I love weddings!

(He dances about.)

COSTANZA: You fool!

ROSINA: (*To Costanza.*) Stop it! You're always humiliating him.

LEONARDO: Guglielmo, before I leave I'd like to clarify the relationship between you and my sister.

VITTORIA: I hope we can sign the marriage contract this evening.

GIACINTA: What good are contracts? Let Guglielmo remember his obligations to Vittoria, give her his hand, and marry her.

VITTORIA: Are you asleep, Guglielmo?

GUGLIELMO: No, I'm not even dozing. Signora Giacinta is right. I have always admired her strength of character; and as the ultimate proof of my esteem, here I am, Vittoria, ready to offer you my hand.

VITTORIA: Because of the esteem you hold for her—not the love you have for me?

GIACINTA: Answer Vittoria. I marvel that you are so grudging and ungracious.

GUGLIELMO: Please . . . don't be upset. I have more reasons than you think. Vittoria, believe me—I recognize your rights. I promise to be a faithful husband . . . and a respectful spouse.

VITTORIA: Everything but loving.

LEONARDO: Enough of your sarcasm. Either give him your hand or I'll put you in a convent.

VITTORIA: My brother makes me laugh. Well, Guglielmo, not compelled and reluctant—as you seem to be—but whole-heartedly and of my own free will I give you my hand.

GUGLIELMO: And I take you for my wife.

VITTORIA: (*Tenderly.*) With a little compassion, at least?

GUGLIELMO: (*Quietly.*) I need compassion too.

TOGNINO: (*Dancing.*) Weddings, weddings, weddings!

FILIPPO: Yes, weddings. When are you going to have yours?

TOGNINO: We've done it already! I'm married! I'm married and I don't care who knows!

COSTANZA: You dunce! You haven't a bit of sense!

ROSINA: I'm glad Tognino said it. You can't hide it. It's bound to be known.

GIACINTA: Heaven grant these newlyweds never regret the easy opportunity for sensual delight they found in the country. I'll say no more, for I know only too well the pleasures I had there and how much they cost me. Thank heaven I'm now married and leaving for Genoa with a mind determined to remember only my duty.

(*To Vittoria.*) I wish my sister-in-law the same peace and tranquillity I desire for myself.

(*To Filippo.*) I ask my dear father to continue to love me even though far away; and if it were not forward and bold of me, I would beg him to regulate his affairs a little more wisely, and vacation in the country more judiciously, and spend less freely.

(*To Fulgenzio.*) I thank Signor Fulgenzio for his good offices. I recognize my debt to him and shall never forget it as long as I live.

(*To Costanza.*) I pay my respects to the mistress of this house.

(*To Rosina and Tognino.*) And I give my best wishes to her newlywed niece and nephew.

(*Softly.*) I salute Signor Guglielmo.

(*Resolutely.*) I'm leaving for Genoa with my dear husband. Before I go, allow me to turn respectfully to those who honor me with their gracious audience. You have witnessed our Craze for the Country. You have participated in our Adventures there, and you have indulged us in our Return. If you have had occasion to laugh at the bad behavior of others, congratulate yourselves on your own wisdom and prudence; and if you are not altogether displeased with us, give us a courteous sign of your acceptance.

End of Play

ROBERT CORNTHWAITE

Robert Cornthwaite was born in St. Helens, Oregon, went through grammar and high school in Portland and worked summers on a farm in the Willamette valley or at Seaside on the Oregon coast.

He was graduated from Grant High with the largest—in fact, the only cash scholarship awarded in his class. He used it in California, first at the City College in Long Beach. By the time he finished at the University of Southern California, a war had intervened and he was working forty-two hours a week in radio while carrying sixteen and eighteen units at the university. With a load like that, getting a Phi Beta Kappa key at graduation seemed unimportant compared to just getting out. The Air Force undertook to broaden him by travel back in the days of Hitler, thus enabling him to learn 5 languages during 3 years in the Mediterranean and other assorted seas.

In 1950 he went into films—making six features that year, including a lead in Howard Hawks' *The Thing*. Nineteen-fifty was also the year he became a Blackfoot Indian. He was adopted into the tribe by Chief Joe Iron Pipe, dressed in feathers and speaking Sioux, all for the greater glory of RKO.

The Thing did just fine at the box office. In fact, it is still screened around the world, and for years it held the late hours of television together almost single-handedly. So for awhile Robert Cornthwaite played scientists, with and without bleached hair, with and without beards, in *War of the Worlds, Futureworld, Colossus: The Forbin Project, Buck Rogers, Yellow Jack, Kiss Me Deadly, Voyage to the Bottom of the Sea, Twilight Zone, Thriller, The Third Man, Hong-Kong*—more than sixty features altogether and perhaps a hundred and fifty play productions.

There were also years of plays as actor and occasionally director in Los Angeles and regional theaters around the country, including New York where he appeared in *And A Nightingale Sang*...at Lincoln Center, *Season's Greetings* at the Joyce and *The Devil's Disciple* at the Brooklyn Academy of Music.

Television took up whatever slack there was from 1953 onward—around two hundred fifty episodes of it culminating in a recurring role on *Cheers* and a regular role on *Picket Fences* until the 1994 season dispatched him forever in a blaze of glory as the demented mayor Howard Buss, nude on a rocking horse.

Mr. Cornthwaite's translations of Pirandello have played at the Arena Stage, Washington, DC; Oregon Shakespeare Festival, Ashland and Portland; Seattle Repertory; East West Players, Los Angeles; San José; Niagara-on-the-Lake and several other regional theaters around this country and Canada as well as the Roundabout in New York.

Smith and Kraus *Books For Actors*

THE MONOLOGUE SERIES

The Best Men's / Women's Stage Monologues of 1993
The Best Men' s/ Women's Stage Monologues of 1992
The Best Men's / Women's Stage Monologues of 1991
The Best Men's / Women's Stage Monologues of 1990
One Hundred Men' s/ Women's Stage Monologues from the 1980's
2 Minutes and Under: Character Monologues for Actors
Street Talk: Character Monologues for Actors
Uptown: Character Monologues for Actors
Monologues from Contemporary Literature: Volume I
Monologues from Classic Plays 468 B.C. to 1960 A.D.
100 Great Monologues from the Renaissance Theatre
100 Great Monologues from the Neo-Classical Theatre
100 Great Monologues from the 19th C. Romantic & Realistic Theatres

FESTIVAL MONOLOGUE SERIES

The Great Monologues from the Humana Festival
The Great Monologues from the EST Marathon
The Great Monologues from the Women's Project
The Great Monologues from the Mark Taper Forum

YOUNG ACTORS SERIES

Great Scenes and Monologues for Children
New Plays from A.C.T.'s Young Conservatory
Great Scenes for Young Actors from the Stage
Great Monologues for Young Actors
Multicultural Monologues for Young Actors
Multicultural Scenes for Young Actors

SCENE STUDY SERIES

Scenes From Classic Plays 468 B.C. to 1970 A.D.
The Best Stage Scenes of 1993
The Best Stage Scenes of 1992
The Best Stage Scenes for Men/Women from the 1980's
Kiss and Tell: Restoration Scenes, Monologues, & History

CONTEMPORARY PLAYWRIGHTS SERIES

Romulus Linney: 17 Short Plays
Eric Overmyer: Collected Plays
Lanford Wilson: 21 Short Plays
William Mastrosimone: Collected Plays
Horton Foote: 4 New Plays
Israel Horovitz: 16 Short Plays
Terrence McNally: 15 Short Plays
Women Playwrights: The Best Plays of 1993
Women Playwrights: The Best Plays of 1992
Humana Festival '94: The Complete Plays
Humana Festival '93: The Complete Plays

GREAT TRANSLATION FOR ACTORS SERIES

The Wood Demon: Anton Chekhov *translated by N. Saunders & F. Dwyer*
The Sea Gull Anton Chekhov *translated by N. Saunders & F. Dwyer*
Three Sisters: Anton Chekhov *translated by Lanford Wilson*
Mercadet: Honoré de Balzac *translated by Robert Cornthwaite*

CAREER DEVELOPMENT SERIES

The Actor's Chekhov
Cold Readings: Some Do's and Don'ts for Actors at Auditions
The Camera Smart Actor
The Sanford Meisner Approach

If you require pre-publication information about upcoming Smith and Kraus books, you may receive our semi-annual catalogue, free of charge, by sending your name and address to *Smith and Kraus Catalogue, One Main Street, PO Box 127, Lyme, NH 03768. Telephone 800.895.4331 Fax 603.795.4427.*